Headlock

Greg McLaughlin

For all my teammates and coaches

1

The world contains two types of competitors; those who hate to lose, and those who love to win.

I live in the camp that loves to win. But while winning gives distinct joy, my truest affection centers around the competition in and of itself. I just love to compete. Win or lose, I'm happiest either deep amid the competition or sweating and straining the preparation to compete. Winning and losing are just the outcomes of that process.

In many ways, I see losing as the necessary dues you pay to learn how to perform better and win the next time. It represents the steps along a journey to develop the knowledge, skill, physical ability and mental endurance required to succeed in the future. Not that anyone is ever content with losing, but I try to extract positives from every situation and focus on how to apply lessons learned from one experience to the next.

Mahatma Gandhi once made a statement that has resonated with me and matches my philosophy about competing and winning. He said: "*I never lose. I either win or I learn.*"

Whether you are the type that refuses to lose or craves victory, few would say they enjoy the process of preparing to win. But that's my favorite part. Games, matches, contests, playoffs and championships come and go. Opportunities in business and life pop up and disappear. You win some and you lose some, as they say. The more you participate, the more you learn what it takes to win. There's the young musician who practices their instrument every day after school. There's the basketball player who shoots 100 foul shots in the school yard after each school day. There's the runner who wakes up early, before sunrise, to put in the miles every morning before work.

The will to win is common. But not everyone has the stomach or the head to put in the effort required to do what it takes to win.

Bear Bryant said it best.

"It is not the will to win, but the will to prepare to win."
I had that will.

In many ways, I've always had it. In other ways, I completely lost it for 20 years.

This is my story about how I found the strength and the willpower to transform myself from a soft, pudgy, middle aged dad to remake myself back into an elite athlete, and how I set the stretch goal to compete in the USA Wrestling Senior National Championship in my late 40s.

2

The clank of the scale jolted me out of an 18-year-long mental slumber. Like awakening from a coma to a loud, jarring stimulus, I watched the arrow quickly rise to the top of the slot without hesitation, bounce once and stick firmly.

My doctor slowly - in my mind as if taunting me - moved his hand over the larger weight and slid it from the 150-pound slot to the 200-pound slot.

"Looks about like 201", he said peering past the narrow glasses at the edge of his nose.

I had crossed a chasm for the first time in my life. I may have weighed this much before, but this was the first confirmed registration of my status as a 200-pound person.

"The arrow is only in the middle of the gap," I said defiantly. "I wrestled in college and when we weighed in, we moved it back until there was just a tiny sliver of daylight between the arrow and the top of the hole. I'm actually a little under 201."

"200 and a half then," he replied.

I subtly sucked in my gut. But when standing on a cold, calibrated scale, your body mass remains constant no matter what gyrations you make to influence the results. We all still do it anyway.

Always a lightweight, the smallest in my high school grade, the only athlete in the school tiny enough to make the lowest weight class, this new plateau came as a shock. And yet, any wrestler or former wrestler has innate knowledge of their body. I knew my weight teetered at the edge of the cliff. I expected to weigh in close. But suspecting it in the back of my mind bothered me far less than seeing it, hearing it and knowing it.

"47 years of age, turning 48 in October," the doctor said quietly to himself as he wrote in his folder. "Five-foot seven inches, 201 pounds,"

"Five-eight," I corrected him. "200 and a half."

"In shoes maybe," he peered at me and smiled. "200 and a half."

"200 flat without the shorts and underwear," I said meagerly, smiling back.

"As a nearly 50-year-old man," he stiffened, pushed his glasses further up his nose and closed his folder, "You need to consider losing weight, or at least holding the line. Without changing any of your habits, you can expect to gain an average of two pounds per year for the rest of your life. That puts you at risk for high cholesterol, heart disease, even diabetes."

"My cholesterol has always been better than average," I said. "I don't have high blood pressure or hypertension. I play hockey three nights a week and volleyball every Tuesday. I'm still quicker and in better shape than most of the 25-year-olds."

The doctor continued as if not having heard my diatribe.

"You should cut back on red meats and sugars," he continued. "At 5'7", or even 5'8" – I guess – and 200+ pounds, you border on ..."

And then he said the word. It sounded like a foul-mouthed insult; a swear worse than any of the major four-letter words.

"... obesity."

I pulled up my pants in disgust and tucked my shirt over my distended stomach.

"You have a couple choices," the doctor continued. "You can cut back your diet, reduce your sugars and eat less red meat. Or you can step up your exercise. The best choice would be to do both. Or, you can always do nothing and just go on medication for the rest of your life like most guys your age."

At home, later that day, I stood in the downstairs hallway facing the floor-to-ceiling mirror between the office, family room and kitchen. I looked deep into my own eyes and tried to find the college wrestler who had dropped 30 pounds to make the 126-pound weight class and win the 1991 Division III New England Championship.

But all I could find was a pudgy middle-aged blob, with greying hair, puffy cheeks, an extra chin or two and a big mound between the pectorals and the belt. This couldn't be the real me. I was never the obese kid. I had always been the slim, slight, little runt, running around like a newborn puppy.

In fifth grade, I wrote an autobiography for an assignment in class. I can still picture the hand-written page stapled to the wall outside the school cafeteria where I listed my height as 4'6" and my weight at 54 pounds. I was small for a fifth grader or even a fourth grader for that matter. In fact, I barely met the average size of the kids two years younger than me in third grade. By contrast the essay written by the biggest kid in school sat just to the right of mine where he listed his weight at 101 pounds, almost double my size.

I arrived in High School as an 88-pound freshman, literally the smallest boy in the class, and not much bigger than the smallest girls either. By my sophomore year in college, I wrestled at a rail-thin 118 pounds. And even by my senior year, I had only stepped up by one weight class to 126 pounds.

But that was 75 pounds ago – or 74 pounds to be precise - and 25 years ago – an average of three pounds per year. I trended my weight gain out another ten years using the doctor's estimate of two pounds per year. I couldn't bear to use my past run rate of three pounds per year.

By 57, I would hit 220. By 67, I'd reach 240. And by 77, I could expect to weigh a whopping 260 pounds. At 5'8", or whatever – 5'7", I'd literally look rounded. Would I even be able to walk at that size? Could I run? At what age would my love affair with playing sports have to end?

My wife's stick-like uncle, who was 6'2" and 165 pounds said something to me years earlier about old people. He told me to look around the convalescent homes and see how many fat people there were.

"They all died early," he said. "It's the skinny ones that live the longest."

So, I formulated a plan and committed myself to Step 1: **"The Food Plan"**. The plan consisted of the following components:
    A.   Cut back red meats and sugars.
    B.   Stop drinking soda and eating ice cream altogether.
    C.   Cut out snacks between meals.
    D.   Drink water all day every day.

E. Reduce portion sizes by at least half.

But, what about the next steps. Would there be a Step 2, 3, 4? I had not completely formulated them yet, but I had an awareness of what they might be, and they would focus on exercising and implementing more physical discipline to compliment the Food Plan.

I already exercised more than many people my age. I played softball on Sunday mornings and volleyball on Tuesday nights. I also played in a competitive adult ice hockey league, two and sometimes even three nights a week with 20 and 30-year-olds who all played in at least high school, if not college. What more exercise could I conduct other than running, which I hated.

In fact, one of the reasons I even believed that my objective to compete in the Senior USA Wrestling Nationals could be possible stemmed from the success I had in my recreational sports. In volleyball, I was still one of the quickest, most athletic players in the league, compared to the other competitors, many of whom were 30 and even 20-year-olds. In softball, I was still one of the fastest runners of all players on every team in the league. I could make diving circus catches that nobody else even attempted. OK, so virtually every team had that one 25-year-old speed demon. But of anyone else, I had as much pop in my legs. And then, there was the hockey league. One could argue that neither the volleyball, nor the softball leagues attracted the highest caliber athletes and that boasting of being the most athletic of the bunch was like claiming to be the tallest Chihuahua at the dog pound.

But the hockey league was different. This was much more intense. Most of the players had played in high school or college. The average age on our team was about 30. In the league, it was closer to 25. I started playing hockey as a four-year-old, but stopped playing when I was 15. I went through a 20-year hiatus and took it back up at age 35. I never played high school or college hockey. And yet, I was still solidly above the average in speed and skills and about fourth or fifth on the team in points scored. Put me in a league of ALL 40-year-olds, and I was sure I would totally rise to the top.

Based on these signs, I convinced myself that with a little added effort, I could be a world class athlete for my age class.

But I knew it would take more effort than I had currently mustered.

I didn't exactly hate running. The reason for my disdain stemmed from what I used to have to do in high school and college to make weight. I used to rip off five, six, seven mile runs at about a seven-minute pace, pushing myself the whole way to go faster, run longer and sprint the last half mile at a sub-6:00 pace. I ran nightly, oftentimes close to midnight, almost always on a completely empty stomach. There were days in college when I lived off a four-ounce glass of water, a piece of dry toast and an orange. And that nourishment had to get me through eight hours of classes, three hours of wrestling practice and a seven-mile run before bed. Needless to say, I had nightmarish memories of both "The Food Plan" and "The Exercise Plan", which I had yet to implement, and which I seriously dreaded.

Part of my problem stemmed from the fact that I couldn't just jog recreationally. I wouldn't let myself. I had too much pride to waste my time doing 10-minute miles in the park or at the high school track. And I despised the treadmill at the gym. I found running in place wedged between an old guy and some yuppie millennial to be a mind-numbing experience. My philosophy about exercise was that if they kept score and named a winner at the end of the workout, I was in. Otherwise, no thanks!

And if I did somehow force myself to start running again, it would be an "all-or-nothing" proposition and I'd push myself to the brink, trying to lower my splits to seven minutes or less.

Committing to a regimen of running for me, would have to become an all-encompassing obsession. I'd have to actually run at a respectable pace, or I would not be able to do it, which is why I dreaded stepping into that territory. But then again, nobody had ever implied to me that I might suffer from obesity either.

I gazed at myself in the mirror one last time and made my first commitment. I have these moments in life where I

7

practice extreme mental discipline. One year, I gave up pretzels, potato chips, Fritos, Cheetos and several other salty snacks for my New Year's resolution. And I went the entire year without touching any of those items. I followed that up a few years later with a ban of all sodas. But when I found myself drinking Snapple and other artificially flavored drinks, I realized that I was cheating the intention of my resolution. So, the next year, I banned them as well. Off and on over the past 20 years, I've alternated between banning soda and other sugary drinks, and then ice cream and then soda again. At least twice, I swore off both soda and ice cream in the same year.

The purpose of these New Year's resolutions was partially about trying to force myself into making healthier choices. I took a food that I abused the most, such as soda or ice cream and forced myself to face the toughest possible challenge I could, head-on. But it was also about practicing my own personal brand of mental toughness.

I have this mental discipline process that I often put myself through. It's the last connection to the total body discipline I've retained from my college days. I pick something hard to accomplish – the closer to "impossible" the better - typically a food-related challenge. And I make a firm commitment to myself. And once I lock that commitment into my mind, I achieve this state of extreme dedication to achieving the objective at any cost. The trick is to find a way to care overwhelmingly more about the ending outcome than about the short-term immediate desires that detract from the objective or degrade the positive progress to the end goal.

As a 14-year-old, I vowed not to swear. I don't know why. But I didn't like the sound of swearing. I didn't like the image it projected. I wanted to be viewed as a nice, upstanding kid. And 30+ years later, I still don't swear, ever.

As a 16-year-old high school junior, I decided that I would not drink alcohol or smoke. These were vices that I saw as pointless and wasteful. And in the many years since, I have upheld that commitment, despite all the peer pressure and social expectations I experienced along the way. I remained resolute. I've never had a drink or smoked throughout my entire life.

I call these pacts with myself "Headlocks".

A headlock is a wrestling move that starts as an upper body throw from the opponent's feet to their back. It is a particularly devastating move in terms of the violence of throwing an opponent over your hips, through the air and flat to their back. The end result is a crushing grasp of the opponent's head and arms that serves as somewhat of a clamping choke hold. Like a bear trap, properly executed, an opponent should never be able to escape a headlock. Few wrestlers in college had a better, more lethal headlock than me. Once I threw my opponent to the mat and locked it, the hold was like a black hole with no way out.

I would take control of my opponent's left arm, by clutching my right arm over it and seizing the back of his triceps. I would draw that arm in and under my right armpit, called an "Overhook". I would then start moving him out of his stance by lowering my hips, shuffling my feet and revolving in small circles. As soon as I felt him edge the slightest bit off balance, I would pop my hips deep into the space between our legs and sickle his neck with my left arm, torqueing his head sideways, pressing his ear against his own shoulder and sinking my left armpit all the way around the back of his neck. The result of this lightning fast reflective move would be that I'd yank his left arm down to the ground, pulling his head with it. My hips, which I positioned between our legs created an obstacle for his balance and caused his center of gravity to remain higher than mine. In sickling the head, I ensured that his ear would remain pressed tightly against his own arm as his entire body flipped over my hips and crashed to the ground.

It's a move that should not work on the most accomplished wrestlers who know enough not to give away arm control and who can feel a headlock coming. There are numerous countermoves to block it. You can duck under my arm as I attempt to encircle the head. You can clutch my waist with your right hand and as we fall to the mat together, you can roll your hips underneath mine, spinning through. Or you can just drop your hips and make yourself too low to the ground for me to elevate.

And yet, I hit more headlocks in high school and college than almost anyone. And out of my several hundred wins between High School, college, Spring and Summer tournaments as well as all the Open tournaments in which I competed throughout my 20s, I pinned at least 100 opponents in headlocks.

In addition to executing the throw, the real secret to pinning my opponents came in the way I finished the move. Most wrestlers cling to the same arm and head that they had controlled while they initiated the move. I do the same until I see an opportunity to clamp down with my own special finish. I like to take the right arm and jack it straight up against my opponent's head and then jam my own head up against his, pinning my ear to his triceps and his triceps to his own ear. From there, I can lock both arms firmly around his neck with no risk of being rolled over.

I've pinned every opponent that I've trapped by this hold. There are actually two different outcomes that I've seen. You either fight it until you can't move and your shoulders touch the mat for the pin. Or you fight it until you pass out, in which case, your shoulders touch anyway. It's happened both ways for me.

The reason I go into such description of my headlock is because I see it as the metaphor for my approach to setting goals and achieving them. Once I decide to make a mental commitment to myself, it's like sinking that headlock finish around the objective and not letting it go until the referee blows the whistle and declares me victorious.

So, I stood in the hallway at my home and made my first set of headlock commitments to myself. I would ban ice cream and soda from my diet altogether. I would minimize my intake of red meat and choose other sources of protein such as chicken or fish whenever presented with the option. I would cut all portion sizes in half. I would only eat food when absolutely hungry, as opposed to some of the mindless snacking I tended to do. And I would avoid any snacking between meals.

This was a pretty aggressive agenda of commitments to make to myself. I stopped to ponder the feasibility of committing myself to this set of goals. I had never failed to uphold such a food-related set of objectives. But then, I had never made such an all-encompassing commitment. I didn't want to set myself up to fail.

I stiffened, restated the rules of my commitments and locked them in my head.

This would be a good first step, and I was interested to see what effect these new tenets would have on my physique and my physical well-being. But I knew there was more to it in the back of my mind. I wasn't ready to commit. I knew to make real, meaningful change, I'd have to do more than play hockey, men's beer-league softball and B-level co-ed volleyball. The day when I would have to lace up a pair of running shoes and hit the pavement would come soon. I could feel it looming. I tried to push it out of my mind. I was not ready for that.

And then another thought came to mind. It was a new thought – one that I was definitely ill-prepared to process or internalize as a firm commitment to myself. But it came to me in passing and stuck in my mind. Could I even entertain the thought? Was it completely crazy? The amount of work it would take to realize this extreme stretch goal would be far beyond my means. And that's what excited me about it.

I looked right into my own blue eyes and asked my soul.

"What would happen if I trained to wrestle again?" I asked, almost out loud. "Could I whip myself into the kind of shape that would enable me to compete at age 47 following an 18-year hiatus? In fact, I'm so much more athletic than guys my age could I realistically compete in the USA Wrestling Nationals for my age group? Could I win?"

I was pretty sure they had a senior division for over 40s, over 50s and so on. But I knew almost nothing about it. I had no clue when it might take place and what the caliber of competitors would be. I only knew that I was way more athletic than almost anyone else I knew in my age group. I still remembered every wrestling move like I had just competed yesterday, and I had a solid history of performing well in big tournaments. But, of course, the last time I had wrestled competitively, I was 28 years old and at least 40 pounds lighter. Could I even last 30 seconds today? Probably, I could not. Could I get there? I had no idea.

I closed my eyes and tried to shake the outrageous thoughts from my head. But they stayed.

"I'm not ready to commit to this," I told myself. "See how the Food Plan goes. Think about running a little bit. But hold that thought about the Nationals. It's a definite possibility to consider."

3

For a little background on me and my sports career, particularly how I started wrestling and progressed through my journey, it started with my dad, Greg McLaughlin Sr. He came from a hockey family and skated on elite teams throughout his childhood. After playing for Hebron Academy, a powerhouse Massachusetts Prep School, he moved on to play for Brown University. In his junior year, he was the high point scorer on the team.

Brown was good to my dad. He met my mom through a teammate, my Uncle David, whose sister, Jane, he eventually married.

By the time I hit 4-years-old, he had me on skates and I played on travel hockey teams throughout my youth as well. I was small, quick and knew the game inside and out. My dad coached me and my teams throughout my entire childhood. By age 10, I was the second highest goal-scorer on our team and had the most assists. I could play any position, left wing, center, right wing and even defense. I won the opportunity to represent my town at an NHL game in the Mini One-on-One competition between periods at the Hartford Civic Center during a game against the Los Angeles Kings. I met hockey great Bobby Orr, shook his hand and even touched the Stanley Cup. And as he walked by me, coming off the ice after the end of the second period, the legendary Gordie Howe, playing into his 50s at the time, cracked me over the helmet with his stick and wished me luck.

Hockey gave me strong leg muscles, great endurance and an instinct to attack and score. While I had a tiny frame, I grew to become one of the most athletic kids in my grade.

The Avon Old Farms private school had a world-class high school hockey team, coached by a former teammate of my dad's at Brown University. Every year, players from Old Farms moved on to play big time NCAA hockey at premier Division I schools like Minnesota, Wisconsin, UVM, Boston University and Boston College. The prep school boasted numerous alumni that played in the NHL including All-Star and Stanley Cup champion Mike Leach of the New York Rangers.

I was accepted to the school coming out of the eighth grade and intended to play big time hockey at Avon Old Farms, but then I broke my dad's heart. All my friends from Avon Middle School were attending the public high school in town, Avon High School. I was young, shy and socially immature. It made me nervous to move on to a new, foreign environment where I didn't have any pre-existing friendships or acquaintances. I told him I wanted to turn down the invitation to attend Old Farms and go to AHS instead.

Avon High had no hockey team, thus ending my decade-long hockey career.

At 5'1" tall and barely 88 pounds as a high school freshman, I had no chance of playing basketball in the winter. I might have been a decent gymnast. But, in reality, I sat around at home watching television every day after school during the winter. For the first time in a long time, I had excessive free time, and I relished the art of wasting it.

One day, not too long into the winter sports season, I was sitting around in Study Hall during the last period of the day. For the life of me, I have no idea where the teacher had gone, but I know we were completely unsupervised for at least 10-15 minutes. The class consisted of a couple freshman friends of mine and some burly sophomores.

The sophomores picked on the freshman and some innocent, playful scuffling occurred. Ever the daredevil, I hopped onto one of the desks, jumped the biggest sophomore from behind, wrapped my arms around his neck and my legs around his back and started choking him. He yelped and tried to shake me off, but with my strong legs, I hung on tightly and probably overdid the choke hold.

The Sophomore, Pete Lindley, was a member of the Avon High School wrestling team. When the bell rang for school to end, he carried me down to the wrestling practice room – I was still wrapped around his back and clinging to his neck.

"Coach," he announced. "I found our new 91-pounder."

As it turns out, I was the only kid in the school small enough to wrestle in the lowest weight class. That moment changed my athletic life and, to a large degree, set me on a life-long path of new accomplishment.

I won my first match four days later, instinctively utilizing moves that I had just learned in practice. Two days later, I wrestled in the Bristol Central tournament, one of the biggest, most prestigious tournaments in the state, and in a shocking surprise, I won first place. I had very few moves in my arsenal, but I benefitted from competing primarily against other freshmen and definitely from my leg strength and toughness. My performance earned me the nickname on the team of "Mad Dog" McLaughlin, a moniker given to me by the senior co-captain of the team, Dave Drago and my idol, senior Rich Hernandez

I finished the season 7-2, won our conference tournament and came in fourth place in the CT State Class S meet. It was surreal to experience such success in such a short time, although losing in the semi-finals showed me a glimpse of what the road ahead would look like. I faced another freshman, Don Nardi, from Nonnewaug High School. He was two inches shorter and covered in real, adult muscles. He dominated me. He squeezed me so tight, I wanted to quit. He pinned me along the way to winning the championship. I had beaten other wrestlers on a mix of natural ability, athleticism and desire to win. This would not be my first tangle with the muscle-bound Don Nardi from Nonnewaug, but it certainly was my least successful effort against him.

Following my freshman year, I started wrestling in spring and summer USA Wrestling freestyle tournaments. I learned the sport better. I shored up my stance. I honed my repertoire of moves. And, I became a pretty effective upper-body wrestler and pinner, meaning, I developed a proficiency for throwing my opponents from their feet to their back and keeping them there until their shoulders touched and the Ref called the pin.

I placed in the State Qualifier and made the Connecticut National Freestyle team that traveled to Iowa every year for the USA Wrestling Junior Nationals.

It was a combination of my Coach Bill Riccio's teaching and my execution at these spring and summer tournaments, coached by the legendary Jim Day, where I perfected my headlock.

I went 15-3 as a 98-pound sophomore and 14-2 as a 105-pound junior, winning the Bristol Central and Conference tournaments and coming in third place in the State Class meet both years. I benefitted from having wrestled essentially an additional season each spring and summer. So, by the time I moved from a freshman to a sophomore, I had the equivalent experience of a junior, by my junior year, I had the experience of a college freshman.

I racked up an undefeated record of 18-0 as a 112-pound senior. I won the Bristol Central tournament for a fourth straight year becoming the first wrestler ever to win that event four years in a row. I won the conference and I won the State Class S meet, beating my muscular nemesis from Nonnewaug High School 6-3 in the finals.

I moved on to the State Open, which combined all the State Class meets into one ultimate State Championship. I took third place, but to this day, feel like I could have - and should have - won. I didn't. I lost in the semi-finals to a short muscular kid, Darryl Stokes, from Norwalk, CT. He went on to lose to Chuck Boyle from Conard High School in the finals. I had beaten Chuckie Boyle numerous times over the past several summers and I am convinced that I would have beaten him had I made it to face him in the finals. But I lost and didn't make it to the finals and he did. I didn't get the chance to wrestle for the title, so I finished third. Chuck Boyle will forever remain the 1986 Connecticut State Open champ at 112 pounds. He deserves it.

I did beat Nardi again 1-0 along the way to third place.

In college, I bounced around and transferred a couple times. It took me a while to settle in to a situation that worked for me. I initially attended Fairfield University, which did not have a wrestling team. I thought I could give it up, but I missed it too much. I then moved home to my parent's house and wrestled for Division I powerhouse Central

Connecticut State University under legendary head coach, Ken DeStefanis.

Needing to eventually leave home for a more complete college experience, I ended up transferring to Rhode Island College, a strong Division III wrestling school just far enough away from home. I weighed about 145 and wrestled in the 118 to 126 weight class range.

Each season, I dropped the 25 or so pounds to compete. But for my sophomore and junior seasons, I had All-Americans ahead of me at 118, 126, 134 and 142, so I could not break into the varsity line-up.

Given this impediment to my personal ambition, I considered transferring again. I even quit the team for a week in my junior year. But I was just running away from an important challenge. And, ultimately, I stayed at RIC to face the challenge head-on.

By my senior year, a spot opened at the 126-pound weight class. This gave me one and only one year of eligibility to prove to myself what I could accomplish. I just didn't know what goals to set.

So, not knowing what outcomes to expect, I set daily objectives for myself to bide time while I tried to define my own upward potential in the sport and on the RIC roster. The goal I settled into was to wake up each morning, make it to every practice first and to be the hardest worker in the room.

This was not a goal that had a tangible finish line or defined reward. It was more of a covenant with myself that I would pursue with blind faith that the effort would pay off at some point before I graduated college or ran out of eligibility. Each day that elapsed without making the line-up was one more day of hard work that I put in toward salvaging my wrestling career, but also one less day of eligibility making up said career.

But I couldn't worry about that. Instead, every day in practice, I would look around, observe anyone who might be working harder than me and then double my efforts to outwork them. I figured that on a daily basis, I couldn't control whether I made the starting line-up. But I could control my own actions and how hard I worked. I kept that faith for three years that the work would pay off. And at the tail end of my college career, it did. Eventually, I formed more specific goals to make the starting line-up and even to win the New England championship once that reality seemed plausible. But it all started with the initial objective to be the hardest worker in the room every day.

As a senior, I earned the starting spot at 126 pounds after narrowly beating the other 126 pounders on the squad in pre-season wrestle-off competitions. I won my first college tournament, the Ithaca tournament, which was one of the premier early-season tournaments in the country. As an unknown, I was seeded 32nd, literally dead last. I caught the first seed of the tournament in my first match. That first seed turned out to be David Hirsch, of Cornell, who, only two years later, ended up winning the 126-pound Division I NCAA National Championship.

I battled Hirsch well. He clearly had more experience and talent than I did. But I didn't give him an inch. I squirmed out of every move he tried on me and kept the score close. With ten seconds left in the match, he had a 5-1 advantage. He could have run away and stalled to win the match. Instead, he wanted to win by an even bigger score than 5-1 against the last seed of the tournament. He shot in on a high crotch takedown and I hit him with an unorthodox move that I learned from Scott Martin, one of the All-Americans at RIC that had graduated the previous year. The move was called the "Worm" and I was able to wrap-up Hirsch with it and throw him right to his back. I held him there for the remaining five seconds of the match to earn the two-point takedown and the three back points I needed to win a near-miraculous come-from behind, last second shocker 6-5.

The win sent tremors across my weight class and suddenly, I had an intimidation factor that didn't exist prior to that win.

I beat the next wrestler 10-9 on another last second score, this time executing a two-point reversal in the final five seconds of the match to transition from losing 9-8 to winning 10-9. I pinned the next two wrestlers using my headlock and found myself in the finals. The final match went to overtime and I won the tournament on an upper body throw to complete the classic come-from-nowhere Cinderella story. I even came in second in the voting for the Most Outstanding Wrestler award.

The tournament win also garnered recognition for me as a "dark-horse" candidate to be included in the top 20 Division III college wrestlers according to the major national college wrestling publication at the time.

It was 1991, I was a 21-year-old fifth year college senior. I had one season of eligibility left to achieve the highest level I could reach. But I did not know what that threshold could be until my coaches, Rusty Carlsten and Tim Clouse, told me that they thought I could win the New England Championship. That became my supreme objective. I won many matches that season, several by pin via the headlock. I entered the New England tournament as the first seed, wrestled as well as expected and made it to the finals.

In the finals, I drew a burly opponent from Norwich Academy, who had wrestled most of the season at the 142-pound weight class and sucked down to 126 pounds to try and take the tournament from me. He seemed much bigger and definitely stronger. When we tied up, he head-butted me in the eye, and my entire face blew up in an ugly purple swollen mound.

They stopped the match and iced it. I could barely see out of it. That didn't stop me. When we resumed wrestling, I tied right back up with him. I took an overhook, used my chest to roll his head into position, sickled his head like a guillotine and hit him with probably the most vicious headlock of my wrestling career. He went straight to his back and I scored the margin I needed to beat him and win the tournament. I didn't pin him as he was strong enough to eventually arch his way out of bounds. But the five-point margin was all I needed to ultimately beat him 8-4.

Winning the State Class S meet and then going on to win the New Englands in college gave me this sense that I could achieve the ultimate happy ending to my goals if I dedicated my whole being to my objectives, focused incessantly on the steps required to get there and stayed motivated in my desire to win, despite the many distractions that life presents. These lessons stayed with me and affected every endeavor of my life from other sports to my social life and ultimately my career.

    I went on to continue wrestling every spring and summer after college out of the sheer joy of competing and the sense that I had a talent and skill that I wanted to maximize while I still could. I racked up dozens, if not hundreds, of medals and trophies. I beat Chuck Boyle a couple more times. I made the finals of the Connecticut Nutmeg State Games, losing a close match to a Division II All American. I won the USA Wrestling Eastern Regionals a couple times and the AAU Eastern Nationals. I even qualified to wrestle in the Regional Qualifier for the Olympic Trials, where I was beaten handily by two Division I All-Americans that ultimately made the Olympic team as alternates.

    I had fun. I experienced great success. I earned respect in the region as an accomplished and admired wrestler

    I also met Shirzahd Amadi. Shirzahd was in his 40s when I was in my 20s. He had wrestled in the 1976 Olympics as a member of the Iranian National team. The first time I wrestled him as a high school senior, he crushed me. But each time I wrestled him subsequently, I did better and by our third match-up, I started beating him. In fairness, he was typically ten pounds lighter than me. But we always had solidly competitive matches. And we both respected each other. We worked out together. He cheered for me when he wasn't facing me. He gave me advice, encouragement and a lot of respect. I admired him for his pedigree and dedication to the sport at an over-40 age. At times, I pictured myself wrestling into my 40s like him. But I never took it seriously. I figured I'd fade out by age 30. And that is basically what happened.

    In my last tournament, at age 28, I wrestled a 20-year-old Division I college wrestler. I was better. I knew I was. By then, I was wrestling in the much heavier 165-pound class. Wrestling while maintaining a 60 to 80-hour full time job and spending all my free time with my new finance made it impossible to control my weight and stay in top shape. At 165, I had the frame and physique of a 135-pounder with 30 pounds of meaningless padding that only slowed my movement and left me much weaker than the field.

In the match, I threw my 20-year-old opponent on his head and took a 3-0 lead. We tied up again. But he was bigger, stronger, quicker and in better shape. I had good position. But he managed to pop his hips into mine, lift me off my feet, throw me and pin me. That match ended my wrestling career at 28-years old. I didn't know it at the time. But marriage, career pressures, bills, eventually kids and a mortgage, would all take me off point from continuing to wrestle each Spring and Summer. Along with the distractions came the additional weight gain into the 170s, 180s and 190s. Late night ice cream, extravagant business dinners, lunches with co-workers and snacks to get through the workday crashed my metabolism, expanded my waist and ballooned my weight.

I stayed engaged in sports, playing hockey, volleyball and softball. But I would focus on career and family for the next 20 years, raising my kids, playing with them, coaching their teams and attending all their activities and events. Their priorities would occupy every spare moment of my time, thought, focus and effort. I hit my forties in what seemed like a heartbeat after passing through my thirties and transformed into the 200-pound middle aged blob that I had become. There was no way I could wrestle again – not with the way I had deteriorated physically. It would take a miracle, or at least an extreme effort to change myself.

I was about to reach deep inside and find that extreme strength.

4

As a manager of a team of millennials all working together to deliver valuable business services and solutions to our clients, I had a mission statement for the team that encouraged them to have confidence in dealing with executives and demanding customers. Our mantra was; "Have Big Vision, a Bold Strategy and a Brave Approach".

The results of my most recent doctor appointment reminded me that I needed to apply that mission statement beyond the workplace and connect it to my own personal life.

After the doctor called me "obese", I kept the conversation with him to myself and neither told my wife, nor my two teenage boys. But for lunch that day, as the rest of the family had roast beef with my favorite A1 Steak Sauce and grilled onions on hard rolls, I opened a can of tuna. I love goopy tuna with excessive mayonnaise and hot peppers on a hard roll, or with melted cheddar on a toasted English muffin, briskly salted. But I kept it light. If I was going to execute the Food Plan, I had to uphold the spirit of it and make real, positive, healthy choices. I ate the tuna on wheat with lettuce and tomato. I added a minimal amount of mayo. It was an encouraging first step and it felt good to make a healthy choice.

But one tuna sandwich on an arbitrary Friday afternoon and a concerted effort to always make healthy choices present two completely different levels of difficulty.

During the week, I'm on my own for lunch while at work in Manhattan. I can control what and how much I eat. We all mostly eat at our desks, so nobody notices if you eat more, less or nothing.

For dinner, my wife provisions the food, but she hates to cook. So, I take the train back, arrive between 6:30-7:00pm and cook most of the meals for the family. With her procuring the ingredients at unawares to my headlock decision to cut back on fatty meats, she still brought home hamburger, steak and sausage on a regular basis. Eating these foods set me back in my objective, but avoiding them at our family dinner table threw up red flags. So, I hedged and ate a little, but tried to fill up on the vegetables and fruits and leave more of the meat behind.

With our kids' sports schedules, oftentimes, dinner takes place at Subway or Wendy's. These fast food places would kill me if I fell into that habit. In these situations, I did not eat at the restaurant, instead opting for leftovers when we returned home for the evening.

I started putting less food on my plate. I subtly cut portion sizes slowly. For one, I had to ease into this new diet. And for two, I didn't want to raise the attention of my family. We had manicotti one night. I casually took a tiny two-ounce piece and filled the plate with broccoli and watermelon. We had filet mignon on the grill another night. Unlike what I would have done in the past, I took the smallest piece for myself and then only ate half of it, offering the other half to my intensely carnivorous sons.

This continued for a week or two, but I could tell that my wife had noticed. And maintaining the ruse was not a sustainable act.

I had to share my decision with the family so that they would understand my choices. So, I spilled the beans. But I didn't just talk about diet, exercise and health. I doubled down on disclosure. And in saying it out loud, the objective locked into my mind and became a headlock.

"I've decided to cut back on my diet and lose weight," I told them all at dinner one night. "I have this crazy idea that I could train for my age division at the nationals in wrestling."

My kids immediately thought the idea was cool, although they also eyed me suspiciously thinking I had no chance to get into good enough shape to survive. I think they pictured me broken in half by some jacked up professional wrestler.

My wife had only one comment for me.

"Don't get so skinny that I have to buy you all new clothes," she said.

Unlike my kids, who know I am very athletic, but never fully experienced what I am capable of accomplishing, my wife had seen me at close to my best. I met her when I was 23 years old and in the best shape of my life. I was wrestling in open tournaments throughout the spring and summer and winning most of them. An accomplished sports journalist and photographer, she came to many of the tournaments, sat mat-side and snapped great photos of me in action.

She's seen me play other sports too and she knows what a gamer I can be. She's seen me place high in road races with minimal training. She's seen me compete with her much younger 20-year-old cousins in touch football and whiffle ball and fit right in as if anywhere close to their age.

We used to compete together in two-on-two volleyball tournaments. Like beach volleyball, most of the tournaments in Connecticut take place at parks on the grass. She played division I college volleyball and has amazing skills. I was a quick, agile, athletic guy who played an awful lot of rec and pick-up volleyball and could hold my own against the bigger guys, many of whom had played high school or even college volleyball.

My wife and I won the majority of our games. We would usually come out of our pool with a 5-1 or 4-2 record, make it far into the playoffs and eventually get overwhelmed in the semi-finals or finals. I don't believe we ever quite won a tournament together. But the experience of playing doubles volleyball with her was intense and exhilarating. We argued and bickered, but we also made each other better and leveraged each other's athletic talents extremely well. Like in marriage, we are a strong team and better as a unit than as a pair of individuals.

We would arrive at the park by about 7:30am and play 8-10 games of volleyball over a 10-hour stretch in the blazing summer sun. I would drink my share of water, but I didn't eat much. Maybe due to my experience as a wrestler, I had learned to play hungry and preferred having an empty stomach. Given the heat and the intensity of the games, I would lose five or six pounds from start to finish at these tournaments, which helped me stay trim and in shape for the wrestling tournaments.

I also played volleyball every other weekend with my friend and regular partner Roger Anderson. Roger was a bigger, taller guy with amazing jumping, spiking and blocking talents. He eventually went on to become a highly successful High School volleyball Coach. Like with my wife, Roger and I also won our pool more often than not and made it to the semi-finals of several tournaments. We finally won a couple after playing together for several seasons. Only 5'8"-ish, it was hard for me to hit the ball hard and straight down the way the six-footers could. I had excellent touch and could place the ball effectively, but Roger had to account for most of our offense. I was so quick and coordinated and willing to throw my body around with reckless abandon, that there were no better defensive players in the area than me. And that was the primary value I brought to our union.

    My wife had seen me wrestle and was well aware of the way I played volleyball, so when I told her that I wanted to wrestle again, she knew where I was going with it and had a good sense of the dedication I would devote to it.
    In addition to her concern that we would have to replace my entire wardrobe, she also worried that I might suffer an eating disorder or that I would contract a skin disease from the other wrestlers. I would have to remind her and reinforce that the tournaments all hire dermatologists to inspect every entrant before the weigh-ins and that anyone with any suspicious skin is disqualified from competition. My wardrobe and skin paranoia became her biggest concerns, as opposed to me pulling muscles, tearing tendons or seriously hurting my neck like I had in my junior year of college.
    Secretly, I worried about the latter.
    I've always boasted that I am made of rubber and can't be broken. Until I hurt my neck in college, I had never suffered more than a broken toe or finger. I always had an extremely high tolerance for pain and as a result, threw myself around in ways that caused people to raise their eyebrows or shake their heads at me.
    My brother, John, was just as crazy and reckless, although considerably less injury-resistant. We used to play "Take-Out" on the hill in front of our yard. The game was barely a game at all. We didn't keep score and there was really no point to the game other than to show off how tough we could be. My brother and I were the only ones in the neighborhood brave enough to play "Take-Out". One of us would stand at the top of the hill. The other stood part of the way down. We

would get a third friend to throw a football out over the decline. The person at the top of the hill would dive out over the drop and try to catch the ball, while the one lower down on the hill would drive his shoulder into the airborne receiver's knees and "take him out".

The game produced spectacular highlight reel wipe-outs. As an adult, I would never let my kids play such a game. Everyone in the neighborhood conceded that it was a miracle neither my brother nor I ever broke our neck or died playing "Take-Out".

But that's how we lived. One spring afternoon, my brother had to climb on to the roof of my parents' house to retrieve a whiffle ball that lodged itself into the gutter instead of rolling back down the roof after I took him deep in our backyard ballpark. Looking down from about 20-feet in the air, my brother inexplicably took a running start off the peak of the sunporch roof and launched himself 30-feet in the air, crashing to the soft muddy ground and nearly breaking both legs at the hard, crash landing. As he lay there writhing in pain, I asked him why he did it, and his answer made perfect sense to me.

"I thought you would think it was cool," said my younger sibling.

As another example of this stupidity, in eighth grade, my brother had a Huffy dirt bike that I borrowed all the time. It was hardly professional grade performance equipment - more your garden variety $59.99 bargain from Caldors. But I rode that piece of twisted metal through the woods, up and down hills, on the beach and everywhere in between.

In the cul-de-sac behind my house, there was a flat circular section of the road, followed by a steep hill fading down and away from the circle. My friends and I set up a horribly constructed ramp made of garbage cans, lawn chairs and sticks with a paper-thin piece of plywood as the incline. We placed this deathtrap in the middle of the downhill. It resembled a poor-man's ski jump.

Nobody would brave the ramp except me. I circled around in the cul-de-sac. My friends lined the hill adjacent to the ramp. I peddled wildly to generate speed and whisked toward the lift. My brother's friend, Markie, tried to stop me but I almost ran him over.

I hit the plywood at about 30 miles per hour. As I rolled over it, the board snapped in half and propelled my body 28 feet - as Markie later measured by tape-measure - down the hill with the bike flailing out of my hands and tumbling past my upended body. I landed on my elbow and left a streak of skin embedded in the pavement. My body went numb. My elbow gushed. The bike barely survived.

My friends had to wheel me home in a little red wagon, as I could not move, with Markie retrieving the Huffy. But I survived with no broken bones. My bike was fine and the event went down in neighborhood history of how crazy, foolish and unbelievably indestructible I was. It also added to my assertion that I am made of rubber and can't be broken.

That feeling of youthful physical invulnerability extended to my sense of mental toughness. Not only did I believe that my body could not be broken, I felt my willpower had the same resiliency as my rubber-made body. So, as I felt hunger pangs from my reduced intake of my mid-life diet program, I separated the emotional discomfort from the physical. I told myself that every rumble and twinge in my stomach represented the digestion process and probably meant that I had lost another quarter pound. This helped take a negative and convert it to a positive.

I applied logic to the process and tried to separate the act of eating based on desire from the practice of eating based on physiological need. In fact, I kicked around my own theories about why people consume food and drink when they do. I categorized eating into five levels of motivation explaining why people eat.
1. **Nourishment**: To feed the body and maintain physical health and strength
2. **Energy**: To get through the busy day that often does not afford many breaks to rest
3. **Social**: To connect with others over a common activity
4. **Taste**: To satiate pleasure impulses that are stimulated by sweet or savory foods

5. **Habit**: To follow time-worn patterns of blindly eating certain foods at certain times

    I convinced myself that I could eliminate some of these categories from my diet. For instance, I didn't have to follow **Habit** patterns if I didn't want to. I didn't need a sweet snack at 2:00pm every day. I didn't need desert every night just because I had always done so. If I wasn't hungry for breakfast, I didn't have to eat just because the clock showed a certain set of numbers or the sun rose to a certain angle in the sky.

    And I didn't have to be a slave to **Taste** impulses stimulated by pleasure centers in the brain. Once you realize that the desire to taste is little more than an instinctual manipulation put on by a series of nerve endings and synapses in your brain, it becomes relatively easy to deconstruct the emotion associated with this temptation. So, if my wife and kids took out ice cream for themselves, I could detach myself from the desire to join them and avoid temptation by reiterating to myself the importance of my end goal. In other words, I saw the bowl of ice cream as a negative influence on my long-term goal as opposed to a positive influence on satisfying a short-term impulse. The problem with satiating these impulses is that they never end and the more you satiate them, the more you experience them. They become a vicious circle that traps many people into a downward spiral toward weight gain and obesity risk.

    When it came to **Social** situations, I realized that nobody pays attention to whether you actually consume food or drink. They simply socialize and consume mindlessly. So, at business meetings, networking lunches and breakfast gatherings, I just took small portions, ate slowly and focused on the social interaction without the habit of eating excessively in the process.

    In terms of eating to maintain **Energy**, I recognized this as more of a physical necessity. I have a full-time job and I can't take a nap in the middle of the day or doze off in meetings. In fact, I had to maintain high energy to perform at my best and continue to meet and exceed the expectations of my employer. However, I also challenged myself to exhibit high energy on less fuel. I tried to gut through the times when I felt tired. I could always sleep on the train or rest when I returned home. It's amazing how little of the food you consume at snack time actually contributes to any meaningful sustained energy boost. In fact, most snack breaks feature high amounts of processed sugar, which operate much like the **Taste** level of eating. They provide a short-term boost, but then create a greater need for another sugary snack soon after. Like with Taste-based eating, Energy-driven eating can also create a scenario whereby the more you snack – on the wrong foods – the more your body signals you to continue to snack. In this way, your mind uses signals and the resulting emotions against you in a deliberate campaign to continuously increase food intake and ultimately stockpile fat. The best example of this points to coffee drinkers. The more they drink their coffee for energy, the more they grow to need it. And then, one day, they find that they have little or no energy until they have that caffeine boost every morning and sometimes several times per day.

    I am not a doctor or a nutritionist, so none of my theories represent any thought rooted in scientific certainty. But I have observed enough to have confidence in some of these concepts.

    I try to force myself to exhibit as much energy as I can without snacking. I try to infuse excitement and enthusiasm in my work. I try to focus on thoroughly enjoying what I do as often as possible. This generates natural adrenaline and allows me to maintain acceptable energy levels on minimal nourishment. I've also turned to snacks such as baby carrots and grapes when I need energy, as opposed to processed foods with high levels of sugar or salt such as chips, cookies or candy, which had been my previous habit.

    So, I managed my diet by eliminating four of the five motivators for eating. At 47-years-old, I had to be sure to consume enough healthy foods to maintain an acceptable level of base health and **Nourishment**. I needed calcium for my bones. I needed protein for my muscular health. I needed vegetables for the vitamins to support my eyesight, my skin tone, my immune system and my heart health.

As indestructible as I still felt, this far along in life, I knew I still had to take care of myself at my age. If I was wrong about this perceived infallibility, the price could be steep. And I intend to live a long life with my family. I couldn't do anything to jeopardize my long-term health. I could survive bumps, bruises, pratfalls and physical exertion. But when you think about heart attacks and other serious ailments that come later in life, even I knew I wasn't impervious to those more serious risks.

I had made some dangerous choices in my youth that could have cost me more than they did. Even so, knowing some of the crazy ways that I made weight in high school and college, both my dad and my wife believe that I would have been a few inches taller if not for the extremities I endured for my sport. I don't completely buy in, but I concede that they could be right.

For the record, I have heard stories of the biggest time wrestlers in faraway places like Oklahoma and Iowa going through far worse measures to make weight. Some kids took suppositories. Some kids threw up. I was always more inclined to simply workout harder and run farther. Although, I can't say all my decisions were perfect.

As a high school senior, I broke my toe a week before the states. It hurt to run. After a couple miles, the swelling pressed against the top of my running shoes and I couldn't keep going. Instead, I went into the school. There was a small area between two doors that had a heater. The idea was that you would come in from the cold, the heater would warm up a small six-foot by six-foot area and then you would enter the school without bringing all the cold air with you. We had figured out how to jam a screw driver into the sensor mechanism and trick the heater into filling the chamber with inordinately hot air. In essence, we build our own little steam room.

So, after running a few miles and working up a sweat, I went to the hot room, sealed myself in a sleeping bag and dozed off in the heat waiting for the sweat to continue to pour out of me. When my father came to pick me up and found me there, he nearly took me off the team on the spot.

In addition to the risk of severe dehydration and possible suffocation, I could easily have passed out and never awoken.

In college, we used to throw on what we called the "plastics", a plastic-rubber suit with tightly sealed neck and arm openings specifically designed to maximize sweating. We would run in the plastics, practice in them and we would spend time in the sauna, also wearing the plastics. Of course, the level of dehydration skyrocketed when doing this.

Sometimes we would remove the plastics in the sauna and watch the water stream out like little rivers. Then we would take our student IDs and for at least 20 minutes, we would use them to scrape off the sweat from our bodies. By removing the bead of sweat from the top of each pore, it allowed the next bead of sweat to formulate that much more quickly. At least, that was the lore. It may have had some basis in science, but we all believed it.

I had found through observation and in learning how my body works, that every time I initially broke out in a sweat, I lost a quarter to a half pound. So, if you can clear the first wave of sweat and achieve a second or third wave, it stood to reason that you could lose up to a half pound each time. Of course, the physiology was much more complex than that, but the system seemed to work.

Some guys chewed gum and spit in a cup in a similar effort to remove as much saliva as possible. That was not my favorite exercise and that's where I sometimes opted to just run an extra mile.

I remember before the Ithaca Tournament in my senior year, I got to the weigh-in and I was still two pounds over the 126-pound limit. So, I threw on the plastics and ran up and down the stairs about a dozen times to work up a sweat. Once I had a decent sweat going, I assumed that I had lost a half pound by working off the calories from running and a half pound from breaking out the sweat, I estimated that I had only a pound left to lose.

That's the way it worked back then. You knew your body so well that you could guess your weight within a half-pound at any moment. You knew exactly which foods you could digest or work off in what time frames. And at the end of a work-out, you could calculate the caloric impact of your efforts, factor any loss of fluid and predict the impact on your weigh-in success within an industrial grade tolerance. I remember flexing my fist and monitoring the muscles up and down my arm. I felt like a machine. I had less than 5% body fat. I could rip off seven miles in about 45 minutes. I could sprint a mile in just about five minutes. I could bang out 1,000 push-ups in ten sets of 100 in less than 15 minutes. I knew every wrestling move, set-up and countermove that existed across collegiate and both Olympic styles of wrestling. Could anyone blame me for this feeling of invincibility?

    I had only ten minutes left before the weigh-in at the Ithaca tournament closed. So, I dragged the exercise bike out of their gym, across their locker room and into the steam room. I didn't care that I wasn't an Ithaca student and that they probably did not want their exercise bike removed from their weight room. I just did what I needed to do.

    In the plastic suit, in the steam room, with sweat gushing from my face, I sprinted a mile on the bike. I got to the scale with a minute or two to spare. I stripped down, wiped all the sweat off my body with a towel that I found in the corner of the wrestling room. I cleared any dust off the bottom of my feet, spit a few times into my coach's handkerchief and stood on the scale, watching just enough daylight shine between the pointer arrow and the gap to be declared eligible to participate.

    Incidentally, I ended up winning that tournament. As mentioned earlier, I was the 32nd seed, basically dead last. It was my senior year. I had been out my junior year with a neck injury having attempted to beat my teammate, All-American Brian Allen, for the starting spot at 126 pounds. So, nobody knew who I was. That was my big opening win against Dave Hirsch from Cornell. And, it sums up why I was willing to subject myself to such torture. It also explains how I gained 75 pounds over the next 25 years. Once I no longer had the thrill of the competition and the motivation to rack up these amazing accomplishments, I had no desire to make those sacrifices either. If I wanted ice cream to satisfy a pleasure impulse, there was no reason not to do so.

But here I was, a middle-aged fat guy. I had just implemented the Food Plan. I had new motivation and a renewed objective. I could feel that I had lost some weight by cutting my diet alone – maybe five pounds down to 195. I felt pretty good about myself. I was about to take on Step 2, "The Measurement Plan" and Step 3, "The Exercise Plan" simultaneously. I hadn't done any running in at least a decade and a half. Could I get back into it and regain some of the fitness I had previously enjoyed? I was about to find out.

5

I had told my family about the overall objective and the Food Plan. I hadn't mentioned the Measurement Plan or the Exercise Plan yet. In order to fully commit to the time and effort it would take to become a regular runner, I needed to find out more information about the objective. I vaguely knew that there was a division for older wrestlers within the USA Wrestling organization. I thought there was some sort of national championship. Or, at least, I assumed there would be. But I didn't know when it took place, how you qualified, who typically entered, what it cost or how the age brackets were determined. I just blurt out at the dinner table one night that I had decided on this goal. And once shared with others, an objective becomes a commitment. At least for me it does.

So, I Googled "Senior", "USA Wrestling" and "Nationals". I learned that there were three distinct tournaments for each of the wrestling styles. There was a Folkstyle tournament, featuring the style of wrestling from high school and college. There were also Freestyle and Greco Roman tournaments, which are the styles used in international competition and the Olympics.

In a nutshell, Folkstyle is a very controlled format, rewarding the ability to take down and control your opponent. Freestyle is a more active format where the rules and scoring model favor quick explosive takedowns and more judo-like throws from the feet directly to the back. Lastly, Greco Roman follows much of the same format as Freestyle, only deliberate touching of your opponent below their waist is prohibited, which leads to even more judo-style throws. Olympic wrestling consists of Freestyle and Greco-Roman formats as they typically entail more spectacular throws and play better on television.

I Googled the tournaments on a Tuesday - April 15th to be exact - and found out that they took place on successive weekends starting April 21st. I had either a week to plan and prepare, or a year and a week.

My age category was actually called the "Veteran's Division" and the birth years spanned from 1972 to 1962, which would be essentially 44 to 56-year-old competitors. I'd age right into the middle of the division.

I looked at the weight classes. At my weight of somewhere around 197 pounds, I'd be a heavyweight in the "Unlimited" category. I could lose ten pounds and get to the 187-pound weight class. Or I could trim down by just under 30 pounds to get to 167.5. For kicks, I looked at the next weight class, 152 and calculated that to be a total weight loss of 48 pounds from my original starting position of 200-even.

I ruled out 152 and set my sights on 167.5. I had a year to train. I segmented a prospective 30-pound weight loss into 2.5 pounds per month over the next 12 months. And when I dissected it that way, it seemed relatively easy, or, I would say manageable. I had already implemented the Food Plan and had some initial success under my belt. I had confidence that I could work my way down to 167.5 pounds in the time I had.

I wasn't positive of my current weight and I wanted to know where I stood and what progress I had made. So, I implemented Step 2, "The Measurement Plan".

In business and in life, the greatest accomplishments come when they are measured and reviewed regularly. Everyone knows how many NBA championships Michael Jordan has won. People who know little about baseball, most likely can tell you who hit 714 Home Runs in the Major Leagues or whether a batting average of greater than .300 is considered good or bad. These numbers have meaning because they are measured, monitored and discussed regularly.

I went out to the pharmacy and bought a digital bathroom scale and benchmarked myself against the goal. I found that I weighed 197 pounds. I had guessed it almost perfectly. I had 30 pounds to go.

Fearing that my kids would want to lose weight like me, my wife asked me to stash the scale out of sight. Growing teenage boys don't need to worry about the number on the scale as long as they eat heathy, exercise regularly and grow at their natural rate.

So, I stuffed the scale under the shelving unit and weighed myself in private every morning and night. I started a spreadsheet and mapped my progress in a chart with a moving average trend line. I took the lowest of my weigh-ins each day and found myself stepping on the scale, three, four and five times a day to try and find the portion of the day at which I weighed the least.

On the Food Plan, I notched down to 196, then 195. The progress went slowly. But I learned a lot about my "float".

Your "float" is the amount of weight you lose naturally over a given period of time featuring regular daily activity. Typically, wrestlers will talk about the weight they float between the time they go to bed and the time they wake up in the morning. The reason the float is important to a wrestler is because if you have to weigh in the next morning at 126-pounds, and you know you float a pound overnight, then you know you can go to bed at 127-pounds and not have to work-out the next morning to make weight. Or you can opt to go to bed at 128-pounds and know that you will only have a pound to work off in the morning.

The float is simply the result of your natural metabolism at work. It isn't constrained to night-time. You can float weight between meals. You typically float less between breakfast and lunch, because there is less time. You might float three quarters in eight hours of sleep. You might only float a quarter in the three hours between lunch and breakfast. Maybe the float would be higher if you are more active in the morning and your float might go up to a half. However, the float becomes negated if you snack between meals. Then you don't know how much you lost versus how much you gained in the snack you ate. Even drinking water disrupts the measurement of the float, because, while water has no calories and is therefore worked off quickly, it still has mass and contributes to your overall weight. So, measuring your float throughout the course of the day is a nearly futile exercise. But monitoring it overnight became an interesting endeavor for me.

As you might expect, I found my float to be affected by the calories I consumed the previous night. A diet rich in low calorie items produced about a 1.5-pound float where a denser dinner only enabled me to lose about three quarters of a pound. I had been aware of this phenomenon in college. But in my older age, I enjoyed tracking and trying to predict it every morning.

And on weekends, I started trying not to consume any food or water between meals and then measuring the resulting intra-day float.

Simply by measuring my weight closely, my motivation to avoid higher calorie foods and eat smartly increased. Like watching your budget every time that you take out your credit card, I thought about the outcome of each eating decision and competed with myself to maximize my float and standardize it at about 1.5 pounds. This fun, competitive challenge enabled me to gain further success and I edged down to 193 and eventually 192.5, all still within the month of April. So, if my objective was to lose 2.5 pounds per month for a year, I had already nearly doubled my quota for April, down five pounds from 197 to 192.5.

I felt a little better about myself, down nearly eight pounds from the doctor's appointment three months earlier. I didn't feel quite as full all the time. I checked myself out in the mirror and thought I could tell the difference in the size of my stomach. The Food Plan in conjunction with the Measurement Plan were working. I was ready to embark on Step 3, "The Exercise Plan".

My kids had correctly pointed out that I would need to be in much better shape to reach the goal of competing in the nationals. And they had a point. I had to run and elevate my wind, my endurance and cardio-vascular shape if I seriously wanted to compete.

So, I threw on my tennis shoes, stretched meagerly and set out to jog around the neighborhood. I didn't even own a proper pair of running shoes. I set my sights on running a mile. My oldest son took the liberty of Googling the route and determined it to be exactly .8 miles. That amounted to about a half mile more than I could comfortably run without experiencing sore knees, tight thighs, hurt feet, searing back pain and tired lungs.

I wanted to stop after the third turn of four, but I had made a headlock commitment to completing the run and I could not allow myself to walk. I slowed my pace and completed the loop in about ten minutes. In my mind, that was enough of the Exercise Plan for one day. But my kids met me in the front lawn with a customized workout agenda cobbled together from their joint experiences on various baseball, soccer, basketball and track teams.

They coached me to ten pushups, ten sit-ups, thirty seconds of planking, mountain climbers, ski jumpers, bear crawls, barrel rolls and a half-dozen other items. Though I needed to sit and nurse my already sore body, I threw on my game face and powered through the 20-minute extreme workout. I didn't want to show weakness or let them down in their enthusiasm to coach their dad.

Fortunately, my wife called us into the house to escape from the early evening mosquitoes and I was spared something they terrifyingly called "White Water Rapids".

The next day's run hurt a little less. My knees held up. My thighs actually felt better. But my back still hurt almost enough to stop me in my tracks, and I didn't enjoy the discomfort in my lungs from heaving for air. Again, my boys ran me through their killer workout as soon as I caught my breath. As much as I dreaded it, I appreciated their enthusiasm and engagement.

The third run hurt about the same as the first two. I wanted to stop, but I would not let myself walk. I slowed to catch my breath, but made sure I kept dropping one foot in front of the other in a running motion. I played the soundtrack from the Rocky movies in my head. I stared down at the pavement watching each foot cross in front of the other. I tried to regulate my breathing and take in deep gasps with my nose and then exhale out my mouth as I had always learned growing up.

And I spoke to myself.

"*Don't stop,*" I told myself. "*No matter how sore or tired, don't quit. It's when you're the most tired and pained that you need to find the will and the toughness to continue. If you quit now, it'll be that much easier to quit next time.*"

Three or four runs later, I managed to survive with fewer aches and pains. My sore back gave me the most difficulty.

Every time I ran, I felt like my lower back had hot acid running up and down my spine.

My wife suggested I buy actual running shoes and we picked up a new brand called Hoka. These shoes had a softer, thicker soul than most and featured a natural curve to help guide the foot forward. As soon as I took my first strides in my new running shoes, I knew the Exercise Plan would succeed. It felt like running on a cloud of whipped cream. I barely felt the road. My feet felt comfortable, like wearing a pair of slippers. My legs felt great and my back stopped hurting almost immediately. I was able to stretch the route to a full mile and eventually to a mile and a half. I added a couple hills and soon found myself able to run about 2.5 miles across to the adjacent neighborhood.

My kids' complicated schedules did not enable them to continue wiping me out after each run. A big part of me felt relief when their interest and availability dissipated. But a small part of me missed it. As the time drew closer, I made a mental note to encourage them to again take up coaching me in my quest for fitness. I thought it would be good for me to work a wider set of muscles and would also enable us to better share in this unique experience.

Spending ten minutes running a mile between arriving from the city and sitting at the kitchen table for dinner time fit my schedule fairly well. But as the distance grew, so too, did the amount of family time impacted by my new activity. Two miles took about 18 minutes, and as I approached three miles, it became more difficult to carve out 25 minutes from our busy days.

The boys had baseball games, track meets, soccer games and music concerts to attend. And I couldn't leave work at 4:30 every day when the rest of my team typically worked through 6:00pm.

I needed a new routine.

My boys generally went to bed around 10:00pm. My pattern with my wife was to relax and watch TV on the couch together until about midnight and then go to bed. Many nights, she dozed off by 11:00pm and slept on the couch until I nudged her and encouraged her to head upstairs to sleep in the bed.

One night, I waited for her to fall asleep. I wrote a note explaining where I had gone and I took off on a three-mile run while she slept. Upon my return, she did not wake up, nor did she even know I had left. I told her about it the next morning and before I knew it, my new routine transformed to a revised schedule of running at 11:00pm.

I had a routine and it worked well for me. I could run three miles consistently at an increasing pace as the weeks progressed. I averaged eight-minute miles, stretching it out on the straightaways and struggling up the two hills near my house.

Most routes I took entailed cruising down the two hills at a brisk pace, followed by a couple miles of straight road. The last three quarters of a mile featured the same two quarter mile hills followed by a last flat stretch to the house.

Some nights I barely made it up the hill. But I always pushed myself to pour my last bits of energy into the straightaway and finish strong. The way I worked out would translate to the way I would wrestle.

In May, I had to leave for a week-long business trip in Oakland, California. The word about business trips is well known. You eat huge meals, go out for late-night steak dinners and spend long days sitting around in conference rooms, munching on candy and snacks while your metabolism slows to a crawl.

I didn't want to lose momentum. I was about to break 190 pounds and didn't want to come back talking about the ten pounds I gained on my business trip like so many of my peers. It would break my heart to see 200 again.

I packed a dozen pairs of underwear, six t-shirts and two pairs of nylon running shorts. I crammed my running shoes into the bottom of my suitcase and committed myself to waking up at 5:30 every morning to run on the treadmill.

As much as I hated treadmills, I appreciated all the analytics provided in the console. I could control my speed and distance. I could check my heart rate, and I could monitor how many calories I had burned throughout the run. I found myself systematically increasing my pace as I approached a mile and then again at a mile and a half. With the insight into how many tenths of a mile I had left before I reached two miles, I jacked the pace and forced myself to endure it.

After each run, I completed 30 push-ups and sit ups. I made a tentative plan to increase by roughly ten each month. In college, I was capable of finishing 1,000 quality push-ups, conducted in sets of 100 over the course of about 15 minutes, I would never return to that outlandish level of push-up fitness. But I wanted to be able to do a couple hundred by the tournament. As my kids pointed out, getting in shape and losing weight was only half the battle. I had to be much stronger.

Throughout the conference, I found it surprisingly easy to avoid overeating. I had no idea what I weighed, but I returned home feeling better, faster and stronger than when I left. After landing and taking the car service home, I grabbed my luggage, left it in the downstairs hallway and shot straight up to the bathroom to check my weight. I pumped my fist in the air. I had hit 188-pounds.

From there, my running distance settled in to a brisk, 15 minutes for two miles. And I managed to run at least four nights a week.

At two miles, four nights a week, I had dropped to 187 pounds, 13 down from my starting point. At three miles, I approached 185. I was averaging between an eight-minute and seven-minute per mile pace. I completely sweat through my clothes. And I noticed that my belt felt a little loose as I was able to use the next hole down from the one I typically used. That seemed like a milestone.

On nights when I ran, late, then weighed myself, showered and went right to bed, my overnight float hit 1.75-pounds and even two whole pounds at times. I had adrenaline levels and a metabolism that I hadn't experienced in a dozen years. I felt great. I pushed myself to four miles, running to the high school and back, and eventually increased to five miles, taking the back roads to the high school and then the main road back.

Occasionally, I felt a strange pull in the tendon that ran along the back of my leg. But otherwise, I felt that runner's high that drove people to long for their next run. I had mastered the aches and pains of running. My legs felt stronger than ever. At night, I would lay in bed, raise a leg into the air and flex all the muscles from my calf, up to my thigh. Most of the fat that had previously filled in the gaps between my muscles, tendons and joints - making them look like big round sausages - had virtually disappeared and each unique muscle had its own bulging definition.

I had mastered the five-mile run. I could complete it at will, pain free. But now, I had to work on pace. I needed to move my five-mile time from 42 minutes down closer to 38. If I could run consistent miles below eight minutes, maybe closer to 7:30, I'd feel like I had reached an acceptable level of fitness for now. Eventually, I'd want to average seven minutes flat.

One of the co-coaches on my sons' baseball team told me about a road race in town. There was a five-mile race and then a few weeks later, a three-mile race at the park by the beach. On a whim, I decided to register. The five-mile race took place on a cool, misty spring day. It was a relatively flat course with one big hill at the four-mile mark. I had no idea what to expect of myself. I hadn't run in a road race since 1999. I hoped to break 40 minutes.

The gun cracked through the air and the racers all took off. I started slowly, unaware of how well I could finish, or even *if* I could finish. I worried about the big hill and wanted to reserve energy to survive it. At least a hundred people ran by me, including the guy who told me about the race. I felt fine. About a mile into it, I had plenty of energy. My legs and lungs felt strong. I stretched my strides and increased my pace. I passed a group of teenagers running in a pack. I edged by a pair of ladies close to my age. I looked up at a steady stream of people in front of me all rounding the next bend. One by one, I passed them all, including my co-coach.

In fact, from the first mile on, I passed someone every 50 yards or so. And nobody passed me.

I took the hill without a flinch and had enough fuel in the tank to sprint the final three-quarter downhill to the finish. Not only did I beat 40 minutes, I finished below 38 with an average mile of 7:35. I felt great. I enjoyed the competition and I couldn't wait for the next one.

The three-mile race took place two weeks later. By then, I had logged another 50 miles running back and forth, to and from the high school at a sustained 7:30 or lower mile. In fact, two nights before the three-mile race, I did four miles in 28 minutes. So, my confidence that I could complete three miles in 22-minutes or so had grown significantly and I set a goal for myself of breaking 22 and dropping into the 21-minute range. The course was basically flat, aside from one quick hill at the beginning. And I firmly believed that I could push myself to a sustained seven-minute pace for three miles if I really set my mind to it.

The race took place at the beach complex in my home town, Greenwich, CT on a beautiful Friday afternoon. There were 275 entrants from all over Fairfield County and Westchester, New York.

This time, I started as fast as I could. I jumped out among the top dozen racers and pushed myself to churn my strides as hard as possible from the opening gun. At the first mile marker, I felt the burn that I had expected to feel in the five-mile race. My thighs strained and my lungs gasped for air. I asked the teenager next to me, as he checked his watch, what our first mile pace amounted to.

"6:33," he told me.

The second mile marker took forever to appear. The teenager was a few strides ahead of me and I was otherwise alone with a couple runners in sight ahead of me and not too many behind me. I had no idea where I stood, what my second split was or how much longer I could run at this pace.

I wanted to slow down, but my headlock commitment to never give in to pain or self-doubt would not let me. Two guys my age strode beside me and we silently pushed each other to maintain our pace. I rounded the last bend sore, tired, heaving for air. I couldn't last much longer. One of the runners around my age was a stride ahead, the other about 12-feet ahead. We all pushed for the finish line together.

As it turns out, I recorded a time of 19:18, which means I not only broke 21-minutes, but I sustained a 6:35 pace for the entire three-mile race. I finished in seventh place out of 275.

The killer was that I came in fourth for my age group. Both of the competitors who finished two-seconds and four-seconds ahead of me won medals and I did not. That detail aggravated me as all I had to do was summon one last surge of energy and will myself ahead. I could have come in fifth overall and second in my age category had I just pushed myself one iota harder to find that last ounce of desire to overcome those two competitors.

I learned two important lessons from the three-mile race. For one, I gained a glimpse at exactly how fit I had become and how much capacity I had for pushing my body up to and beyond limits that I initially thought I couldn't overcome. And secondly, I reminded myself that the difference between "really good", "great" and "the best" can sometimes amount to a 12-foot, four-second difference. To accomplish the kind of goals I wanted to set for myself, I would have to recognize those moments of opportunity and find the strength to push ahead from "good" to "great" and ultimately to "the best".

6

Further research revealed that the New England Freestyle wrestling championships would take place in June. I could register for my USA Wrestling card, which afforded me the insurance needed to compete. And I could sign up for the tournament. It was about a month and a half away. I had broken the 180-pound mark and my weight hovered between 178 and 179 pounds. I felt good, strong, light on my feet and surprisingly confident.

But they didn't offer age categories beyond the "Open" division. This meant that I could face wrestlers in their 30s, 20s and even their late teens including 18 or 19-year-old college wrestlers. Nonetheless, I had no reservations about competing at this level. Sure, I'd struggle to use muscles that I haven't used in years. Of course, the competition would be younger, quicker and stronger. I had knowledge, experience and - I believed - just enough wind, strength and pop in my hips to gut through the physical gruel of it.

As I ran every other night in the brisk evening air, I visualized all my moves. I imagined wrestling through a cadre of young, muscle-bound college-level opponents. I played out how I would tie up with them, what take-down set-ups I would use. I worked through various throws and pinning finishes. In my mind, I understood how tired and worn down the matches would render me and I resolved to try and pin my opponents as quickly as possible to avoid having to gut through too many actual minutes of mat wrestling.

I had executed _Step 1_: The Food Plan, _Step 2_: The Measurement Plan and _Step 3_: The Exercise Plan. And to some degree, I had also initiated _Step 4_: The Disclosure plan.

The premise behind the Disclosure Plan dictated that in order to achieve an ambitious stretch goal, the more friends, family and associates that know about it, the more the people around you can encourage you to accomplish that goal.

For instance, if you make a New Year's resolution to stop drinking soda, but don't tell anyone, then in your first moment of weakness where you take out a bottle of soda and pour yourself a small sip, nobody knows to question you or discourage you from breaking your resolution.

Conversely, if the people around you are all aware of your goal to exercise and lose weight, they tend to ask about your approach and take interest in your progress. You find yourself wanting people to see you making the right choices because you know they are observing your actions, trying to understand how you plan to accomplish your goal and watching for signs that you may falter or fail.

The more people you tell, the more you don't want to publicly fall short.

I had already told my family about my objective to lose weight, increase my fitness and compete in the nationals. I had locked it down in my mind. The time to share it with others had arrived.

I had lunch scheduled with an old friend. We both played college sports. He was a Division I pitcher. We had worked together at a previous company and played softball together. When he went through his divorce, I spent hours on the phone listening to him and helping him through his difficult time. He was a formerly heavy guy that had also trimmed down. His motivation stemmed from a few issues he had with his heart.

At lunch, he referred to himself as having newly become a pescatarian. He ate fish, but no other land-based meats. He said he needed to change his diet due to a series of stints that he had in his heart and the risk of heart disease that he carried with him.

I told him about my Food Plan and Exercise Plan. And I revealed that I wanted to train for the nationals. His face lit up and he wished me the best of luck. He wanted to learn more about it and I explained how the weight classes worked, where and when the tournament would be and how I planned to continue to train for it.

It felt great to tell him and have someone else exhibit nearly the same interest about it that I felt. My kids were excited, but also quite caught up with their own activities. And my wife had considerably more apprehension about it than enthusiasm.

Having successfully told my old friend, I thought about disclosure in other areas of my life. I should tell my brother and my dad. I could share it with my co-workers, the guys with whom I coach my sons' baseball teams and eventually other random dads in town that I saw from time to time.

I worried that people might find this endeavor to be weird. There are still many people who think of wrestling as the sport where guys roll around with each other in tights. I hardly needed everyone in town picturing me in these cartoonish terms. So, I decided to mete out my disclosure slowly, like a release valve.

We had a work team dinner at a New York pizza parlor one night. I hadn't planned on disclosing my story. But for one, my co-workers who see me as often as my family, had already started to notice my weight loss and for two, with all the food thrown before us, a few of them observed my tepid eating habit.

When asked if I was losing weight, I decided to disclose the big picture and tell them about wrestling in the nationals. Their overwhelming interest made me feel pretty good about myself. They asked questions. They wished me luck. Most of the team consisted of young women in their mid-twenties who knew little about wrestling as a sport. They asked interesting questions around who I would wrestle, where the opponents would come from and what I had to do to reach my optimal weight and peak fitness.

One of the girls generated a good laugh when she tried to conceptualize a bunch of men her dad's age wrestling each other and asked the question of the night.

"What do these guys look like?" she said.

"I don't know," I answered. "But if I see any cute guys, I'll give them your number."

So now, in the office, on a fairly regular basis, my co-workers would innocently ask me how it was going. Did I go running last night? How am I feeling?

They also commented on my appearance as I broke the 176 mark and floated down toward the milestone of 175.

"You look great."

"You're getting so skinny."

"How do you do it?"

I had plateaued at five miles and decided to stay with that exact distance as it enabled me to benchmark myself and watch my time drift downward into the high 30's. I changed my focus from expanding my distance to increasing my pace.

The night I broke 175 and weighed out at 174, I threw both arms into the air. I was alone in the bathroom. I had just turned on the shower. I could barely see my reflection in the fog of the mirror. But I felt like I had an arena of fans cheering for me. I had thought it would take the whole year to get down to 167.5. But now, less than 60 days into the process, I was starting to think I could make it in a few months and then maintain that weight for the better part of the year. This would allow me to settle in and get used to weighing in the high 160s by the turn of the year, in time to feel strong at the nationals.

I joked with myself that maybe I should consider continuing to drop down to the 152-pound weight class. But I knew that might be a pipedream and expelled the thought from my head.

Having told my co-workers, I revealed my news to the co-coaches of my sons' baseball team. My wife told a few of her friends.

I visited my dad in Rhode Island and told him. He beamed for me. Always my coach and my biggest fan, my dad spent my lifetime building me up in every possible way. He never missed a game or match or meet of mine. And he certainly never passed up an opportunity to pad my confidence and celebrate my successes with me. I found it heartwarming to share my quest with him and sit at his kitchen table reminiscing about my childhood and all the sports accomplishments our family racked up over the years.

By contrast, my wife turned to me one night and asked an interesting question. The question had a seemingly easy answer. I wondered how she could even ask, although, at the same time, I guess I could see her perspective.

"Why do you even want or need to do this?" she asked. "What do you have to prove wrestling a bunch of kids 30 years younger than you?

"You already had your shot and you won," she continued. "You won the New England championship in college. You have nothing left to prove."

In many ways, she was right.

I compared my sports experience growing up to several of my friends. I had friends that played on a handful of youth sports teams, but never enjoyed the exuberance of winning a championship. They had never experienced the ego boost of being looked at as the best on the team, the best in the league, the best in the state. They had never had their photo published in the paper, holding a trophy. They didn't walk down the street in the center of town and have random kids from school and their parents congratulate you out of the blue for your latest achievement.

That thought presented a strange alternate reality for me as I experienced each of those scenarios throughout my youth and into my high school and even college years.

I had won state championships in youth hockey and high school varsity Soccer. Individually, I was named the MVP in hockey and wrestling tournaments. When I was 11, I won the try out to represent my town at a professional hockey game in the mini one-on-one competition with 30,000 people watching. I won our high school wrestling conference tournament all four years. I was the first wrestler ever to win the Bristol Central Invitational Tournament four straight years. I was also the first wrestler in the history of my high school to finish the season with a perfect 18-0 record. And I won the MVP trophy for the highest point scorer on the Avon High School wrestling team two years in a row as a junior and a senior, also the first to win it more than once.

I qualified for and wrestled in the Junior Nationals every summer throughout high school. I qualified to fly to Pensacola, Florida for the trials for the USA World wrestling team. I won countless regional Freestyle and Greco Roman tournaments every year for about a ten-year stretch including the Eastern Regionals and the AAU Eastern Nationals. In college, I won the Ithaca tournament, beating Dave Hirsch, the eventual NCAA Division I national champ two years later. I even competed in the 1988 regional Olympic Trials as a college sophomore.

After college, I took home a couple hundred dollars in the handful of volleyball tournaments that I won with Roger. My men's league hockey team won five championships over a ten-season period. My co-ed corporate volleyball team won seven championships in 13 seasons. I was named the best defensive player in the league. I have no less than three dozen trophies – real trophies granted for actually winning a competition – and more than 50 medals, all sitting on a shelf in my basement. And, I continued to win major Open wrestling tournaments after college throughout Connecticut, Massachusetts, New York and New Jersey until I was 28-years-old.

My wife was right. I had nothing to prove. But loving to win entails also loving to continue to prove to others - and more importantly to yourself - that you can be the best in any or every endeavor you attempt. I wanted to wrestle in the New Englands because I honestly thought I could adequately prepare myself to succeed. And I wanted to win again, simply because I enjoyed doing it.

I had a few weeks to train for the New Englands. I had broken 170 much more easily than I had expected. Between 174 and 170, I seemed to lose a half-pound on a daily basis. I approached my weight class, only about six months sooner than expected and eventually dropped below 167.5, hitting 167, 166 and even 165.

At one point, a pair of co-workers failed to recognize me after a long weekend having seen me only four days earlier. My appearance changed almost daily. My pants ceased to fit. I had to poke new holes in all my belts and I started wearing my sons' old clothes that they had outgrown.

Not only did my legs look more sculpted than ever, my stomach had all but disappeared. It flattened dramatically and I had the two dents on either side of my actual stomach muscles, which had reemerged after a 20-year absence. My face drew inward noticeably. I had carved myself down to only one chin. And my rounded cheeks deflated like an overcooked soufflé.

People in town innocently asked if I had lost weight. And friends and relatives I hadn't seen in some time, took a double take when they saw me as if not even recognizing me at first.

My wife dreaded the actual competition. She worried I'd break my neck or come home with ringworm. I explained how the mats are cleaned with anti-bacterial chemicals and how wrestlers are routinely checked for skin rashes before each match. The web site for the tournament explicitly stated that there would be a professional skin check. And, after 40-plus years of playing sports, I had barely suffered any injuries, save one hurt neck in college for half of one season.

"I'm made of rubber," I assured her.

She also briefly cautioned me against trending toward anorexia, citing some CNN article about wresters being more susceptible to the disorder.

"I just hope we don't have to replace your entire wardrobe," she lamented.

My oldest son told me one day in the car as we drove to his baseball game together that he was proud of me for losing the weight and whipping myself into shape. It made me happy to hear him express that thought.

"But, you're just not strong enough to wrestle yet," he added. "You've done a good job losing weight and getting in running shape, but now you have to put on some muscle.

As much as I didn't want to hear that, he may have been correct. I had never been a muscular wrestler. I hated lifting weights and avoided it like the plague. For one season, I lifted and built up some muscle during my sophomore year in high school. But I have shunned weightlifting ever since. In college at Division I Central Connecticut State University, we had required weightlifting sessions. I used to purposely arrive late, blaming it on a class overrunning its time and leave early for similar reasons. I'd get in the longest line for a machine and wait until there was one person left. Then just before reaching the front of the line, I'd change my mind and go wait in another line.

Sure, I was probably cheating myself. But bulking up was not part of my plan. I was more inclined to run extra miles, do more push-ups, jump rope for longer than anyone else, drill before practice and stay late for extra instruction.

As a result, I was rail thin, quick, wiry and surprisingly strong for such a slight frame. I won on speed and execution and I succeeded with the matter between my ears. For every move my opponents threw at me, I had two counters. And I had a relentless offensive style, looking to score at every moment of every match, that stifled even the fittest of opponents.

Many wrestlers used a slow, plodding style where they would bide their time, await a mistake, score a point or two and then stall for the duration of the match to cling to their meager lead. Not me. I'm a pinner. Up 2-0, I wanted to reach 4-0. Up 4-0, I wanted to get to double digits. Up 10-0, I wanted to put away my opponent by pin. And if I couldn't secure the pin, I at least wanted to wear down my opponents with non-stop action and constant pressure.

As an example, I observed that every wrestler fights hard in the circle. But as soon as they go out of bounds and the ref blows the whistle to bring them back to the center, virtually every wrestler takes a moment to collect their breath, listen to their coach and straighten out their heads before working their way back into the center to restart.

I saw this as a way to gain a mental advantage over my opponents.

Whenever going out of bounds in my matches, I sprinted back to the center of the mat, crouched down into an aggressive "ready" stance and waited for my opponent to pick themselves up and meet me there. Sometimes I subtly tapped my foot, like I couldn't wait to keep wrestling. Oftentimes, the refs, upon seeing me ready to go, beckoned my opponent to hurry back into the ring.

The tactic frustrated and demoralized anyone who thought they might get a moment to breathe and a few words of encouragement from their coach. It deprived them of the mental break they expected. And it sent a message that I wasn't tired, sore or in any way intimidated and I couldn't wait to keep coming after them.

So maybe my son hit the nail on the head. Maybe I could be out-muscled. But I knew the sport inside and out. I had not lost much quickness in my legs and hips. And assuming I could reach a level of fitness that would enable me to survive six minutes on the mat with younger, stronger opponents, I liked my chances of at least competing admirably.

Plus, I still had my headlock. And I knew I could always rely on that big knock-out punch to pull out a win or two.

7

As I started to feel my body change from slovenly overweight and out of shape, to a more acceptable version of myself, my wife experienced quite the opposite. An accomplished college athlete, having played both Division I volleyball and softball, she had spent the past several years participating in numerous tennis leagues, clinics and tournaments. She had recently moved up from a 3.5 United States Tennis rating to a 4.0.

One season, she notched a 7-1 record for her team. She did not necessarily have the absolute best strokes of her peers, but she outran them all, running them ragged across the court. And when she stepped up to the net to slam her overhead volleys, she did so with a ferocity and intimidation factor that nearly caused her opponents to scurry off the court. She had a reputation as a feared "spiker" of the tennis ball.

But, her 2016 season had screeched to a virtual halt by the time I launched my mission to elevate my fitness. It started with some back pain that she played through for weeks. Eventually, her back hurt so much that she couldn't sit on the couch and watch TV without feeling extreme tightening. She continued to play through the pain until the numbness kicked in. She would wake up in the mornings and eventually in the middle of the night with tingling in her thigh, or along the back of her knees. The numbness moved down her leg and often settled into her feet and toes.

She cut back her tennis days from three to two to one and eventually had to find subs to fill all her spots. She just couldn't play through the pain any longer. She also couldn't find a comfortable position for her body. She couldn't sit without tightening up. She couldn't stand without her back seizing on her. She couldn't find relief laying down either as the numbness took hold of her in virtually every position.

She tried over the counter pain relief medicines, but they didn't help. She couldn't relax, which meant she couldn't sleep. This made her more and more tired and thus, more irritated, frustrated and confused. She had a problem that exceeded the common solution.

I continued my active fitness routine, running late into the night. Often, as I slipped back into the house, I'd find her sitting rigidly at the kitchen table on her e-mail well past midnight.

She'd sometimes ask how I ran. But the more time that went by, the less interest she showed in my journey as she embarked on her own to deal with what turned out to be a serious health concern.

I felt selfish for the hour every other night or so that I stole from her and the family to tend to my own personal objectives, especially since it seemed that each step forward I experienced was matched equally with another step backward by her.

Doctor visits and consultations generally confounded the problem more than helped as several of the initial doctors she visited provided conflicting diagnoses and theories. The first set of X-Rays didn't help either. Not until one of the doctors ordered an MRI did we come to learn that she had a herniated disk in her lower back.

At least we understood the problem. But we still didn't know what to do to fix it. Physiologists that she consulted suggested a shot in the back might alleviate her pain. Surgeons recommended surgery. Both options frightened her – for good reason. The thought of doctors messing around near the vital nerves that run up and down the spine is not a prospect to take lightly.

I tried to encourage her through the frustration and anxiety she felt. But she didn't need encouragement. She needed answers and I had none.

Along the way, I tried to squeeze in the occasional four-mile run here and there. But I always felt a little like a heel for abandoning her for an hour between say, 9-10pm while she dealt with the boys' homework and bedtime routine. I tried to skew my runs earlier in the evening, but that schedule ran afoul against dinner time. I tried to wait for her to doze at night. But most nights, she stayed up well past two am like an angry insomniac unable to comfortably sit, lay or stand and forced to wander aimlessly through the halls as the constant motion provided the only respite for her pain.

I dropped from running 4-5 nights per week to running only 2-3 nights. My total miles per month went down and with it, my motivation and confidence in my objective wavered as well. The nights that I did run, returning past midnight, sweat-drenched and out of breath from some four or five-mile dash only served to highlight the difference in our physical conditions, a comparison not lost on either of us.

One night, my wife managed to fall asleep at 10:00pm in the bedroom. Excitedly, I quickly dressed in my sweats and running shoes and hit the pavement. With the reduced number of free evenings that I found to run, I changed strategies and started trying to dramatically increase my pace. Instead of finishing five miles in 35 minutes, I aimed to break 32.

On this night, I ripped off one of the fastest five-mile dashes yet. I pushed myself from end to end. My legs screamed at me. My lungs burned. All my muscles ached. I could feel the sweat pour. I could visualize the metabolism occurring in my tightening stomach. I knew my opportunities to run were fading and I wanted to make the most of this one.

As I reached the top of the hill in the middle of town and glanced to the left at the return route home, I eyed the option to stay straight, run down to the shore and add another several miles to my total distance. I vowed to make that run some time before the tournament. I figured it would be at least 7-8 miles, maybe even more depending on how far south I swung. But, knowing my wife lay tenuously asleep in her aggravated condition, I took the left and ran straight home.

I smiled to myself as I entered the house, drenched in sweat, heaving in the cold heavy air. I made the slightest of noise entering the front door. A rattling sound and a click of the lock woke my wife from a deep sleep.

In hindsight, I'm sure she would have awoken had I gone to bed with her two hours earlier. I don't believe she was really asleep that soundly. Or if she were, her discomfort would have caused her to stir sometime in the early morning anyway. Even when she did fall asleep, she only stayed asleep for a few hours before the pain needled her awake.

But on this night, she heard the door as she awoke. And as she reached the top of the stairs, her first sight was of me stripping down in the front downstairs hallway, out of my sweatpants and running shoes with my wet hair and deep breathing. And then, I made a horrible mistake.

"Look how flat my stomach is now," I said with the tone-deafness of a narcissist. "I ran hard tonight."

She glared at me from the darkness at the top of the stairs.

"How is your back?" I continued as if an afterthought, following my own glee at my newfound fitness. "Did you get a decent couple hours of sleep?"

It was moments like this that I dug huge holes for myself with my wife. Of course, she answered as anyone in her condition would answer.

"Well, I was sleeping fine until you slammed the front door and woke me up," she said. "But just as long as you can go run so hard and get a nice flat stomach, I guess that's all that matters to you."

I apologized for both waking her up and for blabbing on about my own fitness accomplishments in the wake of her physical difficulties. I had done this before, sometimes marveling at my 20 to 30-pound weight loss and other times almost boasting of the numerous inches I had lost from my waist.

"I don't need to hear how wonderful you are doing with your weight loss progress," she told me some time later. "Don't you think I would like to be able to even take a walk, or sit in comfort to watch TV? Or maybe I could just get a decent night's sleep – never mind playing tennis again? And you're all – 'Look at me, I've lost 100 pounds. I can run 50 miles in 20 minutes …'. It's just a little insensitive, don't you think?"

We agreed that I would not run at night if she managed to fall asleep so that I would not disrupt her precious few hours of rest. And, I made a mental note, despite my own excitement at my progress, to bottle my commentary in her presence as she obviously could not appreciate my good fortune in contrast to her terrible situation.

I'd love to say that I conducted research, spoke to doctors and specialists and led her through her troubles. Honestly, I had taken a new job within the year and the added responsibilities and pressure to deliver on my expanded expectations created considerable stress. It was all I could do to stay on top of my professional commitments, perform the meager responsibilities I had at home including making dinner, cleaning the kitchen and running the evening's errands and still squeeze in the occasional 4-5 mile run to maintain my downward trend in body mass and my upward trend in running speed and distance.

I found myself skipping breakfast daily and eating lunch only occasionally to make up for the reduction in opportunities to hit the road.

With all that focus occupied in those areas, as well as my general ineptitude in managing medical concerns, my wife conducted all her own research, spoke with many of her friends and escorted herself to doctor after doctor seeking the answers she needed for herself.

When she thought about it, I'm sure she resented that I couldn't just handle her health quest for her. But honestly, even if I had quit my job to do nothing but this, I still would not have done it as effectively as her. She just understands the medical world, the insurance plans, the best and worst medical organizations and how and when to seek alternate opinions so much better than I do.

Her options seemed bleak. And finding a doctor to provide a definitive path for her proved difficult.

As I moved forward, she fell back. As I gained strength, endurance and elevated fitness, she deteriorated. As I got IN shape, she dropped OUT of shape. We just seemed to be moving in opposite directions both physically as well as emotionally.

My focus and progress gave me self-satisfaction and made me happy. And by contrast, she experienced frustration, pain and disappointment.

She continued to question the wisdom of spending money to travel to Iowa for a wrestling tournament. She wondered out loud why I cared so much about getting back on the mat. What did I have to prove, she asked me. Why was it so important to me? Why was it more important for me to go running at night than to get a good night's sleep, or to spend that extra time helping her around the house.

To date, the outbursts came in small doses. But I could feel the electricity in the air like the tingling of the skin before a summer thunder storm. The confrontation was coming. She was going to blow soon. And when she did, she could put an end to the whole project, just like that. She had that much power in the relationship. And if she really lost it, I'd have to decide whether to fight and lose or give up to maintain peace. Either way, when the storm hit, I'd lose and probably have to give up the Headlock I had made with myself.

8

With two weeks to go before the New Englands, I weighed between 162 and 164 pounds. I couldn't believe the weight loss pace I had set over the past three months. I counted on losing 2.5 pounds per month. But instead, I was dropping 10 pounds every two weeks. When I broke the 160 mark with about 10 days to go, I decided to try to make 152. At this point, I wanted to hit the mark just as a personal affirmation that I could do it if I set my mind to it.

I assessed my own vitals. I was still peeing daily and I had saliva in my mouth, so I didn't think I had dehydrated myself too much. Back in college, I would go days without urinating and my mouth would go so dry, I made a smacking sound when I spoke. My lips would crack and flake and I could feel my fingers whither. I didn't experience any of those symptoms, so I assumed that my hydration level was at least not at Code Red.

I skipped breakfast and lunch on a regular basis, but made sure I nourished myself at night with vegetables, fruit and just enough protein. I ate a lot of watermelon for the sweet, satisfying juice. I drank about a half-gallon of water a day, usually my favorite - Evian. And I snacked on reduced fat Wheat Thins, baby carrots, almond granola and Life cereal when I needed to munch. Rather than large or even medium-sized meals three times a day, I ate small amounts of healthy, energy-producing foods about six times a day.

I upped my five-mile runs to almost every night for the week leading up to the tournament, averaging five to six nights a week. And I weighed myself three times a day to keep tabs on my two-pound daily float.

I hit 159, 158, 157 with a week to go. My wife watched TV for much of the evening and into the late hours sitting upright in a hard-backed dining room chair. Since I couldn't help her, she told me to *"just go do what I needed to do."* And, thus, I managed to up my running regimen again.

The 152-pound weight class looked like a real possibility.

Then I decided one night to push my mileage. I already felt weary. It was my fourth night in a row running a decent distance and part of me felt like I needed a night off. But I didn't allow it. I wanted to push myself as far as I could. I hit the street and felt moderately strong. So, I decided to stretch my five-mile run up a block or two and make it seven-mile run.

I whipped myself to take the additional hill. I pushed my pace down the back side. I sweat excessively. And I drove my leg muscles to a new level of fatigue. As much as the extra two miles hurt, I commended myself for the mental and physical toughness I displayed in racking up more than 20 miles in four days.

Then I went to the bathroom to weigh myself. I always strip down and try to squeak out some pee before I step on the scale to minimize my weight as much as possible.

As the ounce or two of pee came out, I was shocked at the color of it. As I had reached different levels of dehydration, I had seen bright orange pee and even a brownish color. But this was like nothing I had ever seen. It was crimson red. I had peed about an ounce of blood. I watched it come straight out and then drip down on the white porcelain of the toilet.

I froze, staring at the blood swirls in the bowl. This had to be a bad development for me. I was aware of the risk of losing too much too fast, but I was so sure that I knew my body better than that and understood my limits.

I had a choice. I could report it to my wife, see a doctor and take all the heat that I deserved. It would surely doom my hopes of wrestling in the tournament that weekend. Or, I could eat a little more, drink up and forget making 152, but salvage the tournament. I chose to ignore what had just happened, keep it to myself and maintain my plan to wrestle.

I weighed 155.8, my lowest mark yet. I Googled reasons why you might pee blood. At worst, I had liver cancer, some sort of liver disease, an infection or a severe drinking problem threatening to shut down my entire system. I don't drink ever, so at least I could rule out that possibility.

Best case, I had overexerted myself and experienced leakage from my liver to my bladder. At least one web site referred to it as "*common*" among runners who push their limits too far. In all cases, the Internet recommended consulting a Doctor. If it happened a second time, I would have made that call. Instead, I drank an entire bottle of Evian, had a slightly larger dinner and went to bed without a word to my wife.

Fortunately, the next day, the issue appeared to clear up. I assumed that it was a fluke occurrence and that I was perfectly healthy. I also went right back to my routine, although I took a night off from running.

With two days before the tournament, my wife all but ordered me not to wrestle. She worried about me getting hurt and she convinced herself that I'd contract a skin disease. We argued moderately, but I could tell it was useless to push back. She had dug in her heals and could make life miserable for weeks if I went against her wishes. I had explained that they have dermatologists on site to inspect the wrestlers and that they don't allow anyone with suspicious blemishes to participate. And she knows how malleable my body has been over the years. I simply don't get hurt. But those arguments didn't resonate. And she held firm that if I wrestled, I could sleep on the couch for the next eternity or maybe even move into the hotel down the road.

I spent the day in a foul funk and only spoke to her in short, curt tones. I didn't agree to call it off, but I also didn't take a stand and demand to be allowed to go. I simply walked away from the situation, leaving it nebulous. Despite working so hard to prepare - nearly causing major organ failure along the way - I spent all day stewing that I likely would have to abandon the plan.

And then she called me from the hair salon. Maybe she had overreacted, she admitted. She laid out a few terms. I'd have to be careful and I could only do it if the dermatologist inspects all the competitors. I would have to wear a t-shirt under my singlet to minimize the amount of skin to skin contact. And I'd have to take two showers with a special anti-fungal soap as soon as I returned home. I felt like I had lost a pound of anxiety upon hearing her turn of heart and I had a deep appreciation for her understanding of how much this endeavor meant to me.

With a day to go before the tournament, I weighed 154.8. My co-workers asked if I would be able to make it to 152 with less than 24 hours to go. They wanted to know how I could possibly lose three pounds overnight. I explained about the float. I would fast the entire day and lose a pound and a half before sundown. Then I would drop another pound and a half over night. Inside, I worried that this approach would bring back the bright red urine and threaten my long-term health. But I took my chances.

The next morning at the weigh-in, I made 152 by a hair. That probably turned out to be the biggest triumph of the day.

In keeping with the Disclosure Plan, I told my dad about the tournament and he offered to come watch. I met his enthusiasm tentatively as I had no idea what to expect of myself. I awoke at 5:30am and hit the road by 6:00am. I packed my food for the day including watermelon for the hydration and sweetness it provided. I also grabbed a bag of granola to fill my empty stomach with something heavy and substantial that would take time but minimal effort to digest. The problem with the watermelon was that it would shoot through me. The granola would stay with me and provide energy for several hours. In fact, by eating the granola first, it would block the watermelon from streaking through my system so quickly and hold it in my stomach longer so I could benefit from the natural sugars.

I brought four one-liter bottles of Evian and reminded myself to drink them slowly but steadily. I wanted a consistent stream of liquids flowing through me, but I didn't want to overwhelm my stomach's ability to act as a sponge and absorb the water. I had overhydrated too quickly in the past and it usually ended with me vomiting the contents of my stomach like a Pez dispenser or flushing it out my back end like a faucet.

I brought a ham sandwich to be eaten in the later morning or early afternoon once my digestive system reacquainted itself with the need to generate acids and breakdown foods. I had my Food Plan, I had executed the

Disclosure Plan with my dad and the Exercise Plan miraculously landed me at 152 on the dot.

Now, I had to wrestle. I hadn't been in this situation since the late 1990s. I wore my old singlet from when I was a 112-pound high school senior. I wore my goofy half shirt from college in 1991 and my Rhode Island College baseball cap. I listed myself as a member of the Avon Wrestling Club, a nod to my old high school. And I paid my $35 to participate.

I looked around. Hefty dads close to my age or a little younger milled around with their teenaged sons. Several girls stretched out on a corner of one of the mats. A couple burly dudes with shirts and jackets embroidered "Coach" across the chest strode in and out of the storage rooms setting up tables, warm-up mats and portable scoreboards.

I lay on the soft, spongy mat and stretched my groin. That took a good ten minutes. I pulled my heel up to my backend and loosened my quads. I rolled my ankles around in circles and bounced up and down to get some blood flowing.

A group of ten-year-old boys darted around the gym, chasing each other and tackling their younger brothers on the nearby crash mat. I could have looked around and questioned my sanity. But I didn't. Instead, I focused on preparing my muscles to withstand the abuse that they would inevitably experience. I stared into the distance and replayed my old matches in my head to remind myself of all the options I would have to score points in various situations.

I felt great. I hadn't felt so fresh and energetic in more than a decade. I sparred with the air, pretending to execute single leg and double leg takedowns against an imaginary opponent. I felt quick and capable, a little clumsy, but generally not too far off my recollection of how I felt in my 20s.

I had eaten well and replaced the contents of my stomach with nourishment that would provide adequate energy throughout the day. I drank, peed and drank in a repeated pattern until my body had effectively soaked in enough water to feel completely hydrated. I could feel the blood flow through my veins and fortify my biceps, triceps, quads and glutes.

The gym filled. I picked out a couple wrestlers close to my size that looked older than high school age. The tournament director posted the weight class list and a group of mid-sized athletic guys crowded around to see it. I had not heard of anyone on the list. There were 12 wrestlers in the weight class. Nine of them were in their young 20s with the oldest of them 23. One wrestler was 30. They listed me as 48 years old, even though, I was only 47. I was not the oldest guy in the lot. Unless it was a typo, there was a 49-year-old.

Sure enough, a guy with a greyish beard ambled up to the wall and gazed at the chart.

"You the 49-year-old?" I asked him.

"Yup," he answered with a smile. "You must be the 48-year-old?"

"Actually, I'm only 47," I answered, "I haven't wrestled a tournament in almost 20 years."

"Last year, I wrestled in this tournament," he said. "It was a lot smaller. There weren't nearly as many guys. It was my first time in more than 20 years."

"How did you do?" I asked him.

"I did well," he replied. "I did well at first anyway."

I gave him a look as if expecting him to weave a horror story of getting crushed by the younger opponents.

"I won my first match," he continued. "Then in my second match, I broke two ribs."

For my seeding, which was randomly generated, I drew the 30-year-old first and I saw that as a positive way to ease back into the sport. Rather than tackle the youngest of opponents, I could start off with someone at least a little closer to my fitness and strength.

I drew a former Division I wrestler from Hofstra. He had a whole team of youth wrestlers that he coached scattered about the gym. He was the head wrestling coach at a Long Island high school and he ran the local youth wrestling program. I noted that former college wrestlers who coach are usually in good shape and that the match would likely not be much easier than wrestling one of the 20-year-olds.

That sentiment proved prophetic. The Hofstra alumnus was stacked. An inch shorter, he looked way stronger. His rounded arms and chest took me by surprise as, up close, he looked like he couldn't possibly have weighed the same as me. I shook his hand. The ref blew the whistle and we tied up. I immediately noticed the tightness of his grip on my wrists and my biceps. I fought for control of his arms and had trouble taking any kind of advantage in the tie up. His stance was impeccable and I couldn't move him to set up a takedown, nor did I have much success pushing him off balance to set-up an attack.

He was as tentative as I was, and we sparred with little action for the first 20-30 seconds of the match. I tried to shoot low for a single leg takedown, but I had not adequately set up the move. He defended it easily and I had to scramble back up to my feet before he could counter. As I stood up, he caught me off guard and shot for my legs, sinking deeply and taking away my ability to sprawl and defend the move. I had to go to my stomach and concede the two points.

That's where the match spun out of control for me. He tore me up on the mat, overpowering me with his strength and leverage. I never used to allow my opponents to turn me over my back, but the gap in strength was significantly starker than I had imagined possible.

First, he locked a gut wrench, squeezing both of his arms around my stomach with his shoulder digging deep into my spine. The move is designed to pin my face and chest to the mat while hoisting my hips into the air and allowing him to pry his hips underneath mine like a lever. I couldn't keep my hips down, nor could I muster the strength to remain in a push up position or crawl forward to defend the move. After immobilizing me on the mat and maneuvering himself into position to flip me over, he easily rolled in an explosively quick motion, exposing my back to the mat for two additional points.

Now I was down 4-0. I tried to break his grip with my hands while arching my back to defend the move, but he used his shoulder to flatten me into the mat and executed it a second time. This elevated his lead to 6-0. I grabbed his leg to try and neutralize his advantage and he switched moves to a crotch throw. He simply locked his hands between my legs, pulled me into him, popped his hips up under my chest and lifted me off the mat. I tried to keep my hips down, but his strength completely overwhelmed me. He racked up two more points on the move to up the score to 8-0. One more two-point maneuver and the match would be over on the 10-point mercy rule.

The crotch-throw landed me close to the boundary circle and I astutely swiveled my hips to cross the line. I tried to make it look like I was attempting to execute some sort of move. But the reality was that I just needed to break the momentum and escape the hold. That cost me another point as one of the rules calls for a point awarded to the opponent if a wrestler willingly flees the mat. I was down 9-0, but having gone out of bounds, we could start standing again, where I had held my own.

I had little to lose, down 9-0. I took an overhook with my right arm and tried to move him off balance. I pushed him a little, but not nearly enough. I sickled his head with my left arm and for a split second, I could feel the old headlock start to work. I threw my hips into his and attempted to bring him down to his back.

But I hadn't gained enough advantage in balance. I couldn't torque his head far enough over his triceps and my hips hit his like crashing into a brick wall. He clamped down on me, popped his head free and brought me to the mat for another two-point takedown. I lost 11-0. I didn't score a point. I barely threatened him. And I didn't last the full six minutes - a disappointment to say the least. I had felt so good and strong leading up to the match. I expected to compete more competently.

I practiced what I professed and tossed the loss from my memory. The tournament was a double-elimination format and I had a 20-year-old to battle next. On the positive side, I had nearly hit the headlock and with a little rust shaken off the move, I could envision myself trying it again with better success. Also, I survived that first match with my back intact, my neck relatively pain-free and my arms and legs still energetic enough to give it another try. I had half expected to get partway into my first match and have my entire body give out on me. That didn't happen.

About 20 minutes before my match with the 20-year-old, I watched the guy from Hofstra lose handily to his opponent. That opponent turned out to be my next opponent.

The 20-year-old, a recent graduate from an exclusive private Prep School in Connecticut, crushed me. I couldn't maneuver him any more than I could move the 30-year-old. He toyed with me for a minute and then grasped my arm in a Russian tie-up. I immediately executed a spin move to escape and take a shot at his legs, but he stopped me easily, scoring a two-point take-down along the way.

Then he tied me up in a gut wrench and turned me over my back almost at will. It took him about a minute to rack up points and beat me 10-0 mercilessly. After Googling him, I learned that he had placed fourth in the Prep School national championships only a month earlier.

I had survived the tournament. I had no idea that the caliber of competitors would be so high. I was outscored more than 20-0. And my back hurt for the next month.

In all, I focused on the positives about having worked down to the weight class and survived against the two monsters I faced. When I started my journey, I had a goal to lose 25 pounds down to 167.5. I exceeded that goal by 15 pounds, nearly doubling my expectations. I also aimed to reach a level of fitness that would allow me to compete in actual tournaments. I had accomplished both goals.

But my sons called it correctly. To compete seriously, with any chance to win – or at least to score a point - I needed to focus on my severely lacking strength. In addition to my plans around Food, Measurement, Disclosure and Exercise, I needed <u>Step 5</u>: **The Strength Plan**.

9

The downside of the Disclosure Plan is that you have to update everyone and answer all their innocent questions along the way.

"Hey, how did you do in your tournament," asked everyone on my team at work.

"Well, I didn't win," I replied. "I didn't wrestle in my age bracket, since they didn't have the older age group at that tournament, so I wrestled in the Open division against 20 and 30-year-olds."

That reply told the story succinctly and gave people a good picture of why, after all that effort, I had not seen more success. I positioned it as a part of the training process, like running with ankle weights so that once you remove the weights, you feel stronger and faster.

My kids immediately reinforced their earlier feedback that I needed to bulk up and increase my strength and my wife quite bluntly told me that I had gotten it out of my system and didn't need to keep doing it. She suggested that I had experienced so much success with my running, that I should continue to boost my health while focusing on road races and developing into the best, most successful runner that I could be.

Even my dad, who had always expressed pride in my effort, referred to my performance as "*kind-of*" wrestling. I knew I had to have looked my age. For my dad, whose favorite adjective is "*terrific*", to provide less than glowing feedback for the first time that I could remember, I must have looked old, slow, weak and bad.

When I asked him if I looked at all like the old Greg at any point, he replied, that I definitely looked like an *old* Greg.

In the days following the tournament, my weight spiked a few pounds to 158, but I was surprised not to have exceeded 160. I immediately went back to my Food Plan eating sparsely during the day, avoiding snacks and focusing on heathy choices. I also jumped right back into the Exercise Plan and completed my five-mile runs four nights per week. Within days, I stabilized my weight in the low 150s, floating back and forth between 155 and 153.

Prior to the tournament, I had attempted to build some upper body strength by doing push-ups after my runs. When I started, I could rip off 10 push-ups without too much trouble, but I felt the strain on my pectorals after conducting 20. By my business trip in May, I had improved to an easy 30 with the muscular stress kicking in at 40. Just after the tournament, I completed eight sets of ten without feeling any tightness or soreness. Soon after, I hit 100 and by the Fourth of July, elevated to 125 conducted in five sets of 25.

In college, we used to do what we called the ladder. We would complete 10 jumping jacks, push-ups and sit-ups. Then we would do 20 of each, then 30, 40 and 50. Once we reached 50, we would descend back down the ladder, finishing 40, 30 20 and finally 10. The total number of reps came to 250. I made this one of my new strength goals.

I belonged to a gym in town, but had worked out there only once with my son. In fact, I didn't even work out. I just sat in the massage chair and supervised him. If I were going to gain strength, I would have to find a way to build another half hour into my schedule. And with the gym hours running 6am-8pm, I would have to make further changes to my daily routine. I would have to relegate the strength plan to the weekends, miss my kids' weekday baseball games or find an alternative in the city near my office.

So, I had identified five steps in my journey. In addition to *Step 1*: **The Food Plan**, *Step 2*: **The Measurement Plan**, *Step 3*: **The Exercise Plan**, *Step 4*: **The Disclosure Plan** and to a limited degree, Step 5: **The Strength Plan**, I now needed to practice the sport of wrestling. As much as I could envision moves and counter moves in my head, I could not pretend to have all that muscle memory readily available at such short notice and at the hair trigger required to make them all work in the live environment. And any modicum of success in men's hockey or coed volleyball did not adequately translate to quickness on the mat against the younger opponents I faced.

I should have known what to expect when, before the tournament, a 180-pound wrestler asked me to warm up with him by drilling moves. As I hit my single and double leg takedowns, my duck-unders, my arm drags and my fireman's carries, I felt awkward. My balance wavered, and my form lacked the smoothness and grace I exhibited in my 20s. I never afforded myself the chance to test out my form in the live matches. And, as a result, I struggled to execute a viable setup and failed to complete a single move beyond fighting in vain to avoid exposing my back to the mat.

I conceded the need for _Step 6_: **The Workout Plan**. And by "Workout", I specifically meant working out in a wrestling room, practicing moves with a partner. I would have to research wrestling clubs in the area and figure out where the 20 and 30-year-olds practiced. I'd also have to build that into my work and family schedule, balancing it against my need to conduct my strength plan and continue running 5-6 miles every other evening. My head spun with the depth of planning and time management this crazy Headlock pact with myself would require.

One of the biggest hurdles to the entire program slept next to me every night, washed my laundry every week and drove me to the train station each morning. I would have to persuade my wife to allow me to attend wrestling practice in the evenings between my 40-minute runs and my new strength training regimen.

I held off from mentioning it and quietly limited my eating to maintain a trim 153 average. I continued running 3-4 times a week and raised my push-up and sit-up tally deeper into the mid-100s.

I researched road races and resolved to build up to a half marathon by the end of the next summer. Maybe next fall, I would think about training for a full marathon.

But I didn't want to push too far ahead in my thinking or my long-term objective planning. My priorities consisted of running for endurance, firming my muscular fitness and finding a way to improve or at least refresh my actual wrestling skills.

In researching wrestling clubs, I came across another tournament scheduled for the end of July. I had played volleyball and wrestled in the Connecticut Nutmeg Games as a 23-year-old recent college graduate. Our volleyball team won the championship. And in the wrestling tournament, I took the Silver medal, losing a close match to a Division II All-American from Springfield College.

I could weigh in at 158, or I could drop to 149. Again, the only available division for me would be the Open age group, so I would face 20-year-old recent high school and college graduates. But the two appealing attributes of the Nutmeg Games for me consisted of the fact that only Connecticut residents could participate and the style of wrestling would be "Folkstyle".

Limiting the pool geographically might strip out big names like 30-year-old from Hofstra, who hailed from Long Island and the 20-year-old Prep School All-American I had faced in the Freestyle New Englands, who also lived in New York and had accepted a scholarship to wrestle at UPenn.

Folkstyle wrestling better matched the format I wrestled throughout high school and college. I would have a more realistic shot of performing respectably in the Nutmegs. I had a better grasp of reality and understood the odds against winning the tournament or even winning a match. But I saw it as another chance to execute a couple moves, maybe score some points and compete admirably.

I didn't need to win. I just needed to go through the process of learning how to compete with the physical tools my mind and body had to offer at this stage. And I wanted to further benchmark myself against the trajectory I had to follow to prepare myself for the Senior Nationals next April.

According to my wife, this dream had died, and wrestling again had dropped off the table of possibilities. So, I needed to delicately introduce the idea, let it fester and then hope for another miraculous turnaround at the last minute.

Another problem that I faced existed deep within the muscles running along either side of my spine. They hurt. I had huge knots on both sides and at times could barely stand up straight. I hid this pain from my family to avoid having to own up to their skepticism of my choice to follow this path and their inevitable pronouncement of *"told you so."*

But sitting at work all day felt like daggers digging deeply into my tissue. Waking up in the morning required just the right technique to roll off the side of the mattress and catch my balance before falling on my face. Pulling on socks or tying shoes required enormous effort and pain resistance. The worst experience came when I sneezed a few times. The activity nearly knocked me off my feet, with my entire body shuttering in pain.

Every chance I could find, I lay flat on the floor and stretched. I leaned back against the doorjamb to deliver my own self massage. I pulled my arms across my chest and over my head to loosen the knots. I rolled back and forth across a thick Styrofoam exercise tube. It took several weeks, but the pain started to dull. After each run and subsequent piping hot shower, I felt better. Another tournament would set me back again. But I didn't care. Like a mother entering her second childbirth, I blocked the memory of the pain from the last experience in anticipation of the excitement of the next one.

But I still dreaded the conversation with my wife that loomed on the horizon like a dark foreboding storm. I resolved to tell her about the Nutmeg Games one night, but our schedule kept us running from place to place, dropping off kids at their activities, picking them up, feeding them and helping them with their homework. Another night, I waited until the kids went to bed, but by the time I approached her, my wife had nodded off on the couch as well. One night, she had a dinner with her friends until late at night and upon her return wanted to tell me all about it. And on a fourth evening, as I prepared to broach the subject, she got mad at me for finishing her box of cereal and not telling her. Or was that the evening that she yelled at me about the laundry? Or maybe that was the time I forgot to feed the kids before I left for my board meeting.

It seemed that every night I intended to reveal my new plan to wrestle, a roadblock popped up causing me to hold off for another night.

Finally, one evening as she folded laundry, I sat at the top of the stairs and told her that I wanted to give it another shot.

She looked at me, paused, made a slightly sour face and then took a breath.

"Alright," she said. "If that's what you want to do, go for it."

And that was it. I had the green light to engage in round two of my quest to compete. I couldn't believe how easily the conversation played out and I, again, appreciated her understanding.

Maintaining my weight had grown more natural to me and I broke 152, hovering down into the low 151s and even breaking that plateau to about 151.2. I had a few weeks to go. I regularly banged out 125 or more push-ups. I was running a hard five miles on a regular basis. I was even finding ways to eat small lunches and breakfasts and still maintain my weight. And, four weeks after the New Englands, a good 90% of my back pain had finally dissipated.

I had a few business dinners scheduled and a trip to San Francisco that I would have to work through. But I had no doubt that I could make it to 149 and compete at that weight class. I was down to two or even one meal a day with 3-4 small healthy snacks. I would have a handful of granola for breakfast and some fruit. For lunch, I would snack on baby carrots and low-fat Wheat Thins with a clementine flavored sparkling water. Around 3pm, I'd have more Wheat Thins if my stomach hurt from hunger. Beyond that, I avoided any other intake during the day. In the evenings, I ate whatever dinner the family had, but I cut the portion size in half. After dinner, I snacked on handfuls of Cinnamon Life cereal and drank limited amounts of Evian water to stay meagerly hydrated. I liked to reward myself with two double stuffed Golden Oreo cookies, pealing them apart and making a single quadruple stuffed treat for myself. It was my one indulgence per day that I allowed.

This eating regimen continued my downward trend and propelled me into the very low 150s.

And then one morning a few weeks before the tournament, I awoke at 152.4 after a day where I had a business lunch and an after-work event that I had to attend. Knowing I had gained from my average, I skipped breakfast. I had a relaxed business schedule for the day and decided to work from my home office. I had a gap in my calendar from 10am-11am and decided to run in the heat of the late morning. It had to be 95 degrees and muggy. But I flew through the run. I sweat buckets in my nylon shorts and long sleeve cotton t-shirt. I managed to squeeze in a shower and weigh myself just before my 11am conference call. I had hit a ridiculous new low – 148.6 – the lowest I had weighed since the age of 25. I had already made weight for the Nutmegs and just had to stay there. I could focus on strength for the next few weeks and try to increase my chances of winning, or at least scoring a point.

The web site for the Nationals, which would take place in six months, listed the weight class below 152 as 138.5. I allowed myself to entertain the thought. That would be a mere ten pounds more to lose over the next 200 days. It would also represent a 65-pound loss from my starting point of 201. I stashed that thought and shielded it from the Disclosure Plan. I was not ready to go there. And if I allowed myself to lock up the thought in a new Headlock pact with myself, then I would have to go for it and I would start to tell people about it. I dispelled the thought and it left my mind – mostly.

As an interesting aside, I ran into a former co-worker at a restaurant a few days after hitting 148.6. He looked at me and recognized me immediately. But he took a double take and started to comment on my appearance. He seemed to want to ask if I had lost weight. But he stopped himself. I believe he thought I might be sick and didn't want to bring up a sensitive topic. I quickly told him that I had worked out and changed my diet to lose weight and he responded that I looked great.

My transformation had been so quick and stark, I realized that people who had not seen me in more than three months might start to think I looked seriously ill.

As I dropped below the momentous 150 mark, my boys decided they wanted to work out with me. My older son started weighing himself occasionally and trying to cut back on some of his snacking. He ran a half mile here and a mile there, around the neighborhood. He asked me about my workout plans and told me that he had lost a few pounds. He, and my younger son also resolved to join the high school Cross Country team in the Fall to further whip themselves into shape like their old man had done.

My older son asked me to go to the gym with him for a more formal workout. The younger one decided to join us. They wrote up a workout plan and texted it to me. They structured it quite intelligently. Their regimen included a half mile warm-up run on the treadmill at about an eight-minute pace followed by 10 minutes of stretching. Then, they opted to run a half mile at a seven-minute pace followed by 10 push-ups, 10 sit-ups, 30 seconds of planking and 10 leg lifts. They planned to repeat the workout three times in a row, followed by a half mile cool down run. By the end of the session, they would have completed two miles on the tread mill, three sets of 10 on their exercises and a minute and a half of planking.

I cut each of their exercise times and amounts in half for their initial workout, but left their running plan intact. I ran alongside them, but they would not let me do the push-ups or sit-ups with them since I could do them so much more smoothly and easily and it made them feel bad to see me outpace them so dramatically.

They worked hard. They didn't cheat or scrimp on their exercises. They ran their distance diligently and completely. They encouraged each other. I admired their efforts with pride. And I felt like a good dad for inspiring them, even if just a little bit, to push their bodies into a better level of fitness.

We looked in the mirror standing side by side. My older son had me by two inches and at least 50 pounds. The younger one was maybe a half inch shorter and about the same weight. But what stood out to me was our muscle tone. I had definition, but significantly less mass than they did. They had rounder muscles with definitely more baby fat. But in many ways, they looked healthier. You could see my collar bone and ribs much more clearly. Certain tendons in my neck stuck out more pronounced and gangly.

I had to shift my focus from weight to strength. I had six months before the nationals. If I could cut down to about 145 and then gain back seven pounds of muscle, I would look phenomenally fit and healthy. And I'd minimize the chance of being overpowered and outmuscled as I had been at the New England Freestyle tournament.

I resolved to add curls, bench press and a few other standard weightlifting exercises to my growing routine to round out my Strength Plan.

I had reached my weight class for the Nutmeg Games. I had my wife's blessing. I could rip off 100 push-ups at will. I had made a lot of progress since the New Englands. The Nutmegs would give me another benchmark milestone. But I already knew what I needed to do if I wanted to become a national champion. Simultaneously while I continued to cut down, I needed to bulk up and round out my muscle tone. And I needed my boys to continue to inspire me as they had at the gym that day.

10

A week before the Nutmeg Games, my wife re-expressed her reservations about my plan to continue to wrestle. I could see her conducting her own mental wrestling matches in her head, trying to balance her support with her concern. She didn't stand in my way, but she sure appeared uncomfortable with the idea.

Also, the playoff schedule for my boys' travel baseball teams came out and they both had critical games on the same day as the wrestling tournament.

"Go ahead and wrestle," my wife dripped with sarcasm. "If that's more important to you than your kids' baseball playoff games, then I guess you have your priorities set."

Now I had the opportunity to grapple with my own mind. I hated the idea of missing their big games. But I had worked so hard to prepare for the tournament and I could not bear to miss it. There would not be any other tournaments that I could attend between the end of the summer and the beginning of the next season, which would mean that this was my only chance to compete before the Nationals next April.

If I wanted to know where I stood, it would be now or never. And granted, the Nutmeg Games tournament would only represent a second data point in conjunction with the New England Freestyle tournament the previous month. But at least two data points could formulate a line and indicate a direction. I had to know if I could perform better this time compared to last time. I would risk disappointing my wife and missing my kids' games. Secretly, I would hope for rain. But I had to compete. I had to know.

My wife softened her dialog and helped me out quite a bit the day before the tournament. I decided in my typical last-minute style that I would like a new wrestling singlet that fit me better and a set of protective headgear to help avoid the cauliflower ear that many wrestlers developed as the result of burst capillaries around the earlobe. I stopped by a few sports shops in New York, but couldn't find what I needed.

My wife found a small, medium and large at a shop in town and picked them up for me.

The Medium fit perfectly and I looked much less ridiculous than in the Youth Large I had worn at the previous tournament.

The rain teamed on Saturday night before the Sunday morning tournament and all the baseball games washed out. I went to bed weighing 147, two comfortable pounds underweight. I had fasted the whole day eating only one small piece of mozzarella cheese for dinner. I could have eaten much more, but I hated that anxiety of cutting it so close and wanted to show up at the weigh-in worry free.

In hindsight, I should have eaten more. When I stepped on the digital scale, I could not believe the number that popped up on the LED display -144.5. I was 4 and a half pounds under for a total weight loss of 55 pounds in four months

It didn't matter that I came in light. I ate my watermelon and my granola. I hydrated, stretched and tried to pick out the competitors in my weight class. I felt ready to wrestle and stronger than the previous tournament. I thought I could win. I really did.

For my first match, I drew a 27-year-old. He looked enormous, covered in tattoos and felt like he was made of brick. I later found out that he was a former Connecticut State Champion who did not wrestle in college, but who had since become a semi-professional mixed martial arts fighter.

We shook hands. We tied up and the experience reminded me of wrestling against Pingtafore in the New Englands where I couldn't control his hands or move him off balance. He gripped my wrist and biceps and I could feel my arms bruising in his clutch. He squeezed so hard, I couldn't move. But technique-wise, he was not materially better than me. Essentially, I could wrestle toe-to toe with him and possibly even score on him.

He took me down with a high-crotch shot that I almost stopped. I sprawled and hit him with a hard cross-face. His strong arms pulled my left leg in close to his chest and I had to bail to my stomach to avoid going to my back. With me face down on the mat and him on top, he went to work, abusing me for the next minute. He drove his head into my kidney while trying to curl my knees into my chin for a cradle, but I kept my near hip down and my legs extended straight. I arched and flexed my back to avoid buckling as he tried to fold me in half at the gut. He reached up under my head and powered a strong half nelson over the back of my neck using my upper arm as a lever to turn my head and attempt to roll me to my back. I looked away from the half nelson, chopped down on his arm to alleviate the pressure and avoided keeling over. He switched from move to move, reacting to my defenses. He next hit me with a vicious cross face, raking his forearm past my nose and mouth and grabbing my far triceps. He pulled it under my body, doubled up on it and pounded his shoulder into my back to flatten me onto my forehead, face down on the mat. I was still able to turn my hips away, crawl up to a base, get a leg out for stability and stop his attempts to turn me.

I could stop him. But I couldn't escape.

The first period ended with him leading 2-0.

At the start of the second period, he won the coin toss, which afforded him the choice of starting on top of me or on bottom. A wrestler will typically select bottom as it is easier to escape than to hold a man down. So, starting on bottom often equates to somewhat of a free escape point. He had the added choice of deferring his selection to the third and final period, leaving me to decide whether to choose top or bottom in the second.

"I'm definitely not choosing bottom," I said to the ref as I stood there pondering my options, and the two minutes of brutality I had just endured.

"I wouldn't either," he whispered back to me with a smile.

My opponent had dominated me to such a degree, that choosing down would no doubt doom me to spending the entire second period fighting off more bruising cross faces and cradle attempts. Choosing top would almost surely give away an escape point. At only 2-0, every point would matter greatly, if I believed I had a chance to win the match. I chose neutral and took my chances that I might be able to take him down from standing. If anything, I could attempt a headlock and try to knock him out in one big move.

There would be no headlock. He took me down on a single leg takedown about 20 seconds into the period. I tried to hook his far leg and execute a punishing split leg move called a spladle. But I wasn't strong enough to hang on to his leg or yank it forward into my chest as I needed to do. Again, I had to base up, yielding him two more points, to avoid giving up even more back exposure points.

And then, down 4-0, I scored my first point in 18 years, a one-point escape. I managed to take control of his wrists and stand up, despite his weight bearing on my back. I didn't have time to enjoy the accomplishment as he came at me immediately and nearly took me down again. I held on until the end of the period to defend his attack and finished the second period only down 4-1.

I had to assume the top position to start the third and final period as my opponent chose down, presumably to earn his free point. Surprisingly, I rode him well, covering his hips, chopping his arms to the mat and keeping enough pressure on his back to make it difficult for him to get away. Apparently, I still had some effective technique in the top position within my dusty repertoire of moves. However, my opponent worked hard to escape and my newfound ability to stay on top did not last.

As I started to lose my control over him, I remembered one of my brother John's favorite moves, called a Zook. I slipped my left leg inside his right and locked my foot around his ankle, like an inside grapevine. I grabbed a nearside head and arm lock and attempted to stretch him forward. The idea would be to eventually roll under his chest pulling his legs, hips and head over my body and exposing his back. I squeezed it with as much strength as I had to give and stretched him forward. I could hear him groan a little bit, so I knew I had the move well executed. We struggled against each other for quite some time, neither able to improve their position. He fought with his strength. And ultimately his fortitude trumped mine. I couldn't hold on and he scored a two-point reversal to go up 6-1. He immediate went back to his cross face, bruising my nose and scuffing a chunk of my cheek. I managed to escape again close to the end of the period and lost by a respectable score of 6-2.

I stood in the lobby outside the gym trying to catch my breath. My arms hung down by my side in exhaustion. I contemplated eating my ham and cheese sandwich and drinking another bottle of Evian. I had too much adrenaline flowing to adequately feel how stressed my back and neck muscles were, but I could tell that it would be a rough morning the next day.

A heavy-set guy my age, maybe a few years younger, walked right up to me with his hand extended.

"I admire you," he said. "A bunch of us were pulling for you. I don't know how you do it, going out there against these 20-year-old kids. It was an inspiration to see you battling that guy so tough. Nice job. Hope you win the next one."

His wife pitched in her own praise and asked if I was Ok. It felt good to earn the respect of random spectators even in a losing effort. Another person overheard the exchange and contributed well wishes for my next match.

"You're representing us older guys," he said. "Everyone was watching you out there."

I ran into a tall, athletic-looking middle-aged dad in the bleachers. I instantly recognized him as Ken Pera, a throwback to my own high school days. Ken was a state champ from our biggest rival, Berlin High School. We had wrestled together on the Connecticut National team and I had coached against him after college. He had since moved to my home town, Avon, and worked with my brother to run the town youth wrestling program.

He took a double-take when he ran into me. He never expected to see me in a singlet on the mat again. It was nice to chat with a peer, who had seen me in high school and held that deep-seeded respect for my body of work that others use to exhibit, back when I was a more relevant figure in the Connecticut wrestling scene. We reminisced about guys we both knew in high school. I asked about Coach Day, the legendary coach at Berlin High, who had also served as my coach on the National team.

At the start of my second match of the day, I saw Ken work his way through the crowd and take a seat on the side of the mat.

That next match popped up too soon. I had maybe 25 minutes to rest and replenish. Then I drew another former Connecticut State Champ, a college sophomore who wrestled at the University of Virginia and won his conference championship earlier that spring. He was nearly as strong as the MMA fighter, although considerably less intimidating. At least he didn't have knuckle tattoos.

But what he did have was the ideal combination of strength, speed, quickness and agility. He looked like an extraordinarily muscular gymnast and moved like a boxer, bouncing up and down, back and forth, always on the balls of his feet and ready to pounce.

When he hit me with his double leg takedown, his execution was flawless. His head drove straight into my sternum and he yanked both of my legs out from under me before I could react. I was down 2-0 in seconds and again fighting off my opponent from the bottom position. But this guy's style differed greatly from the MMA fighter. He took control of my wrist, hooked a leg and conducted a move called a tilt. Not so much designed to result in a pin, it generated three points for exposing my back to the mat.

I managed to return to my stomach from the tilt and worked to get back to my feet. When I stood up, I hooked my arm over his in a whizzer position, using it to secure my balance on my feet. He used his underhook position to gain leverage and hoist me off my center of gravity. In a split second as I rose from the mat, he popped his hips underneath mine, threw me straight through the air onto my head and pinned me. He hit the throwing move so quickly and exploded through it, I had no chance of stopping it. My feet soared through the air as my body rotated over his hips and slammed to the mat with a loud slapping thud. I heard the crowd gasp. The ref smacked the mat to signify the pin. And, just like that, I had lost again.

I shook it off. He just caught me off balance with a good move. It happens. I hadn't been pinned in 25 years prior to that match. But it didn't bother me.

"*I never lose*," I thought to myself, quoting Ghandi. "*I either win or I learn.*"

And I had just learned the danger of letting a young quick, opponent drop his hips underneath mine. I reminded myself to be more careful in upper-body throwing situations.

In my third and final match, I drew a kid who wrestled at the Naval Academy, but was not a starter. He was also on the Navy Jujitsu club. He was built somewhat like the wrestler from Virginia that had just pinned me, quick, strong and athletic. He took me down and rode me for a minute or so, but I managed to reverse him with five seconds left in the first period to tie the match at 2-2.

In the second period, he chose to start in the down position, hoping for a quick and easy escape point. But I dominated him from the top position. I threw my legs over his hips and wrapped them under his legs in a double grapevine move that enabled me to stabilize my hips on top of his while keeping all my weight pressed into the lower half of his spine. It stopped him from being able to stand up and escape. It also gave me freedom to work on his head and neck and try to turn him to his back.

I executed a power half nelson, controlling his arm, neck and head and managed to torque his ear sideways enough to turn him toward his back. I used my legs to squeeze the life out of his stomach and freeze him from rotating his hips to escape. I scored three points for exposing his back to the mat and took a 5-2 lead. After he squirmed out of that move, I hit him with a double chicken wing that tied up both arms behind his back. Using his arms as levers, I rotated my hips all the way around his head which flipped him upside down behind me and exposed his back a second time. I scored three more points for the move to up my lead to 8-2. I thought I had him pinned, but I ran out of time in the second period to stick both shoulders to the mat. I chose the down position and stalled most of the third period. I escaped once to make it 9-2 and he took me down with about 30 seconds left in the match to reduce my lead to five points. But he couldn't score any additional points and I ended up winning by the final score of 9-4. It was my first win since the late 90s. I ended up taking third place in the tournament.

I sat in the bleachers for an hour after that third and final match of the day, waiting for them to announce the place finishers in my weight class. It's funny, but at 47-years-old, having won literally hundreds of matches and nearly as many trophies and medals, I was still excited to earn and receive this medal.

I showed it to my kids and my wife and all three of their faces brightened with pride. It reminded me of the feeling as a teenager when my parents would beam at my accomplishments.

It didn't matter that I couldn't straighten my back, or that I had little round bruises dotting my arms and shoulders or that a small chunk of my cheek was missing or that I had an odd, misshapen bruise across my nose from the numerous cross-faces I had endured.

I had won a match against a 22-year-old college wrestler. I walked away from that tournament – or rather, I hobbled away – feeling like I had taken an enormous leap forward in my goal of preparing for the Nationals. And I had positive news to disclose at work.

Just in case anyone doubted me, I received a text from Kenny Pera with a series of pictures he had taken. There was one with me turning my opponent to his back with my leg scissor and power half. And there was another, which I set as my laptop background photo of the ref holding my arm in the air to signify my victory.

11

I took a week off after the Nutmeg Games. I wanted to jump right back into my rigor, but I needed to give my body time to recover. My back hurt nearly as much as it did after the first tournament and the range of motion in my neck had many of the same limitations and sticking points.

And yet, the pain was not as deep after the second tournament as the first, lasting for approximately one week instead of three.

My weight stabilized, bouncing consistently between 145 and 149. I could eat a little more than I had, and remain in that target zone. I heard about a couple more tournaments in Massachusetts over the next few months. I wanted to set my sights on them, but we had a busy Autumn coming up with school starting, my older son's college search and application process and the upcoming Fall baseball season. If another tournament worked out, I would go for it. But I had pushed my luck and maintained good will at home. I had to pick my battles.

I wrote a long e-mail to Jay Jones, my former college teammate, now the coach of the Rhode Island College wrestling team. I laid out my whole story for him. Now that I had won a match, I could confidently unleash the Disclosure plan on anyone in my circle of friends including my extended network of associates. Jay served as the central nervous system of the alumni network, so telling Jay about my exploits equated to sharing the news with everyone from my college days. This new exposure would further elevate the pressure to stay on track.

I doubled down on my Strength Plan. I didn't want to just impress my old teammates simply with my new lean physique. I wanted the total body. I wanted to look the part. I wanted to look like the national champion I aimed to become.

I started at the gym doing curls and a few other lifting exercises. I also sought to complete the ladder; finishing 10, 20, 30, 40, 50, 40, 30, 20, 10 push-ups in succession during the course of a single workout. I had done a baby ladder completing 5, 10, 15, 20, 25, 20, 15, 10, 5. I figured it would take me until the start of the tournament in Iowa to build up to the feat of completing the ladder. But as I had done in estimating my ability to lose weight, I also overestimated the timeframe for completing the ladder.

One night, in mid-January, I watched the movie *Creed* as my wife dozed next to me on the couch. I always experienced great motivation from the Rocky movies. I stood in the hallway with no shirt staring into the mirror. I bounced up and down as if preparing to wrestle. Like I had done at the start of my journey, I stared deep into my own eyes. I liked the chiseled face that stared back at me.

I dropped for the first set of 10. I stood up and pointed at the skinny guy in the mirror, daring myself to complete the ladder right there and then. I banged out the next set of 20 without breaking a sweat. I took a minute to rest and then breezed to 30. A few minutes later, I finished 40 push-ups, struggling through the last 10 in the set. The burn started to seep into my pectoral muscles. I bounced in front of the mirror and shook out my arms. The adrenaline overwhelmed the pain. I finished my set of 50 on the way to ramping down to 40, 30, 20 and finally the last 10. The push-up total reached 250 in one shot, conducted over about a 15-minute time duration. I could hear the Rocky theme song in my head. Energy seared through my veins. I flexed and threw my arms in the air like the Italian Stallion himself. If I could have, I would have sprinted the steps of the Philadelphia Museum of Art.

Completing the ladder seemed like another major milestone. I sent Jay Jones another e-mail asking if I could work out with his college team at least a couple times in the winter to help in my preparation for the Nationals. He wrote back that he'd love to see me on the mat at RIC and I added this "to-do" to my newly formed Workout Plan.

My wife's back continued to turn for the worst. Some nights she had to go to bed at 7pm, lay under the sheets in discomfort and stare at the ceiling all night unable to sleep. Other nights, she climbed out of bed and wandered through the house unable to find any comfortable resting position other than to remain upright and in motion like a zombie in the dark. She sat rigid in a hard wood dining room chair, called out to our Amazon Alexa and passed the time listening to books on tape, since it hurt too much to lay in bed and hold a book out over her lap.

The physiologists suggested a cortisone shot in the spine. The Cardiologists all recommended surgery. She fretted over this decision, conducting tireless research, consulting her friends and parents and seeking second, third and fourth professional opinions.

Throughout her ordeal, I squeezed in five-mile runs whenever I could. I pressured myself to run as fast as possible to maximize the value of each workout. A slowly-jogged five-miler 2-3 times a week would not maintain the pace of physical metamorphosis I had set over the previous five or six months. During the late Summer and early Fall, I saw my average mile drop from nearly eight minutes to much closer to seven. Every night that I managed to pull away from the family, I aimed to complete the five-spot in precisely 35 minutes and came darn close on numerous occasions.

I dreaded the winter as I'd have to find a way to maintain my weight and my discipline despite the biting cold. Would I still be able to go out nearly an hour at a clip and run in the sub-freezing weather? Would the snow and ice make it too difficult to run outdoors? And how much would Thanksgiving with my family and the Christmas week, spent half with my in-laws and half with my siblings set me back. I envisioned the great physical shape I had achieved slipping backwards and resolved to remain focused on a day-by-day basis until the weather turned for the worse.

I wrote an e-mail to my former college coach Rusty Carlsten, to share my story of fitness, obsession and madness with him. As a coach, I adored Rusty. He saw my potential and encouraged me to stay with the team throughout my difficult underclassman years when I did not make the starting line-up and contemplated quitting. He had an interminably positive attitude and affirming nature that simultaneously comforted me and drove me forward. He had a vision of what he thought I could accomplish and a way of helping me see the best version of myself. It was Coach Carlsten that first suggested I could win the New England championship well before I ever set foot on the mat as a starter. He helped me believe in what I could accomplish with the right amount of effort, practice, patience, experience and will.

I wrote him a long e-mail, detailing how the doctor had derided me for my bloated weight. I told him about that first three-quarter mile run and the rapid pace at which I had shed the pounds. I gave him the play-by-play of my five wrestling matches over the course of the two tournaments and I laid out my plan to train for the nationals. His reply beamed with pride and encouragement. And, I gained further confidence in my mission having shared the plan with him. I promised to keep him posted and he expressed excitement at hearing the updates from me.

Until I corresponded with Coach Carlsten, I had identified two major challenges to my overall plan. There was the guilt of taking off and leaving the house a couple nights a week as my wife lay in agony on the bed, unable to sleep or even move with any great ease. And there were the growing demands of my challenging job as Senior Director of Business Automation Solutions at the Ad Tech start-up in New York City. Rusty added a third insidious concern to the list.

"Just remember," he wrote. "*At your age, the biggest competition may not be the other wrestlers that you face, but the constant risk of injury between now and the start of the tournament. Take care and be careful of your body.*"

As I contemplated the increased pressure I would feel as a result of the impending cold winter months, I started to worry about overdoing the miles, pounding my knees too harshly on the rock-hard pavement or pulling a muscle in the increasingly cold air. I thought about slipping on a patch of ice or twisting an ankle in an unseen pothole in the dark of the night. As much as I felt like I was made of rubber, I conceded his point and recognized the fragility of my journey. At any point, a simple injury could end the whole endeavor. Or at least I could face a devastating enough set back such that making any reasonable weight class could fall out of reach. As quickly as I had lost 45 or 50 pounds, an extended period of inactivity due to injury could cause me to gain it all back quicker than I cared to admit.

I had never commuted to New York City throughout the course of my 25-year career. We had specifically moved to Greenwich, CT, along the Metro North railway line in case I ever needed to find corporate employment. I had always worked in Connecticut and driven to my office along Route 95 North in my car. But for the past year, I had relied on both Metro North and the New York subway system to get me to my new job on 23rd and 5th at one of the leading Advertising Technology firms in the world, deep in the southern bowels of midtown Manhattan and the beautiful Flatiron District.

The job rocked. I had a great team and we took on major business improvement initiatives, launching significant revenue-producing projects with increasing success. The 80-minute commute took some adjustment. But the excitement of the job overcame any downside of the longer commute time. It did, however, make squeezing in my 45-minute workouts that much more difficult. Family dinners floated toward 8pm. With my wife's back agony, I spent 9pm-10pm cleaning the kitchen, carrying laundry up and down stairs and running errands necessary to get the next day started. I often found myself hitting the street at 11:00pm, even 11:30pm some nights. After returning past midnight, I often didn't get to sleep until close to 1:00am.

If my wife had managed to fall asleep by the time I returned, I didn't dare climb the creaky stairs to join her in our bed. So, instead, I would take the couch and sleep there the best I could. This happened several nights per week. I knew it couldn't be good for my back. And I understood that I wasn't getting quite the deep sleep I needed. Coach Carsten's injury warning weighed on me. But I had no choice. If I wanted to put in the miles, this was the only way to do it.

So, my typical day started at 6:30am, where I would roll off the couch to make scrambled eggs for my boys and a fried egg for my wife. I'd quickly clean the pans and put away the dirty dishes before jumping in and out of the shower by 7:15am. Sometimes my wife would drive me to the Riverside train station. Other times I'd ride my bike or walk the two flat miles. I'd work all day, allowing myself a four-ounce bowl of granola for breakfast and a two-ounce handful of reduced fat Wheat Thins with a two-ounce bag of cold, wet, sweet baby carrots for lunch. This would give me just enough energy, sustenance and vitamins to get me through the long day. By 6:00pm, I'd walk three blocks to the subway with my stomach grumbling and tightening. I'd remind myself that the dull hunger pain represented the natural calorie-burning process and looked forward to weighing myself before dinner to see how well I had metabolized my eight ounces of easily digestible food.

My wife took care of provisioning the ingredients, but I cooked the meals. The task typically occupied my sole focus from 7:00pm to 8:00pm, with clean-up and errands lasting well past 10:00pm. I've always had great energy, so the limited sleep in combination with the active schedule did not slow me at all. The biggest difficulty stemmed from my wife's continued physical deterioration and the growing frustration she experienced.

As guilty as I felt leaving her to run, I still did it. I had to. And I know, she didn't always understand how I could make that selfish choice to prioritize my own physical enhancement over what she perceived to be a lack of caring for her situation. But I rationalized – fairly I believe – that there was little to nothing I could do to ease her suffering. And sitting around the house with her would not serve either her nor my purpose.

Maybe she resented that I could pursue an athletic objective and she couldn't. Maybe there was more I could have done to help her through her issue. Maybe she just needed my companionship during those times when I was absent from her side. She clearly didn't always seem to fully grasp why this wild goose chase of mine meant so much to me. And probably, she experienced a combination of all these emotions.

The bottom line was that when I needed to, I left and somewhat selfishly took care of my own fitness objectives.

And as much as I worried about the impact on our relationship, I also did it unapologetically. A big part of me wanted her to care as much about my ambition as I did. I figured I could mend any jealousy, resentment or hard feelings after the tournament. But as time unfolded and her physical condition worsened, so did the tension between us.

As if the stress of my professional grind and the strain of my wife's herniated disk issue did not make my Headlock commitment challenging enough, my oldest son would graduate later in the year and we had to help him apply to colleges throughout the early Fall. This process, as it turns out, can become a time suck. It can drain all your attention and sap every ounce of energy from your body and mind. The amount of research required to truly understand how to maximize your chances of acceptance at your stretch schools soon consumed my wife and son. I tried to pitch in. But I had little spare time between managing the breakfasts and dinners, my commute, the workload and my wrestling prep.

My wife spent her days on the internet reviewing all the application rules and procedures. She and my son spent countless afternoons planning his essays, helping him edit his ideas and fine tuning his grammar and word selection. We visited campuses, attended open houses, networked with alumni and corresponded with key Admissions professionals and staff at his target schools.

My wife spent hours thinking through strategies and coordinating with my son. I tried to help. But I just didn't have the time to devote to it that they did. As a result, I was more of a bystander and a gofer, helping with smaller, more tactical aspects of the overall strategy. I helped edit the essays. I proofread applications and I rode along on the campus visits. But, for the most part, despite her excruciating ordeal, my wife found the strength to lead my son through the process.

This made it harder for me to take off and go running at night or retreat to the basement for 25 minutes of push-ups and sit-ups. I had to read the tea leaves and determine when to abort. If we had a pressing deadline or a critical challenge to overcome, I scrapped any thought of allocating time to working out and buckled down to help with the application process. On the nights that I did leave the house, I did so with a weight around my neck, knowing that the family left behind - in some way - might have resented my focus on me during this trying period of intense devotion to my son's future.

I also experienced a major setback in my job right around the time that all the college application deadlines started to hit the calendar. My boss pulled me aside and gave me a heads-up warning that the company would be conducting some major actions to reduce staff and that my job would be affected. For the first time in my life, I faced the possibility of unemployment. We hadn't saved enough – or barely any of our money for that matter. As if my wife's horrendous back pain issues had not placed enough strain on our family, now, I had to deal with the uncertainty of my employment, my career path, my income and the financial security of my family.

Probably the biggest fear was the realization of how much we needed the healthcare coverage. The cortisone shots, the prescriptions and - God forbid – any decision to engage in surgery would exceed our ability to pay out of pocket. I needed to devote my attention to the job search and devote my sole focus to that over any other family priority – including the Headlock commitment to training for the Nationals.

I had until the end of the year to find another job. I felt confident that I could find *"a"* job. But could I find *"the"* job that would enable us to continue our lifestyle as is? That question weighed on my mind.

I turned 48 on October 30th facing a barrage of challenges. I was not at an ideal age to be in the job market. I needed a top of the grid salary to maintain our cash flow and with the nature of my expertise, the range of open and available jobs would be extremely limited.

My wife had finally decided to get the cortisone shot and it had failed miserably to provide any relief. Essentially, the doctor missed the spot and she experienced greater pain than she had before the procedure. I was a month into this period of career uncertainty. And we had seven college applications due within the next 15-days. This entailed multiple essays to complete and a myriad of decisions to finalize. Then, once we hit "*Send*" on the college application site, we had to apply for financial aid and start to plan how we would pay the exorbitant bills we would ultimately see six months later.

On a positive note, I still managed to maintain my hectic schedule and get out onto the road about three nights per week. I was pushing the mile count past five, hitting six and even seven miles per workout. And, I had stabilized my weight at 142 pounds, only three or four pounds over the 138.75 weight class for the Nationals.

But, I had to find a new job. We had to finalize my son's college applications. And my wife needed her back problems resolved. She hadn't had a decent night's sleep in more than five months. She was grinding herself into the ground with the college process. And my self-driven focus on my physical training was causing a wedge of tension between us that I would have to eventually address with either a confrontation that I would surely lose or a tacit retreat, which would most likely damage or even end my quest to participate in the tournament. Something had to give. And it had to happen soon.

I took stock in my progress and the road ahead. I had started at more than 200 pounds and couldn't even run a full mile only six months earlier. I thought about the nagging back problems that my wife faced and the strain it imposed on our entire family, including the tension in our relationship. I observed all the stress and uncertainty of my career peril. And my 47 years of age had just flipped to 48, reminding me that I was only getting older and my life was only growing more complicated. I longed for the days in college when I had no family to manage, no bills to pay, no job responsibilities to uphold and virtually no limitations to the direction I could steer my life. If only I had found the same level of focus, determination, vision and discipline then that I had discovered now, I might have won the National Championship as a college senior. And maybe I wouldn't need to do what I was trying to do at this ridiculous stage in my life.

And yet, with all the challenges I faced at 48 years young, I still experienced growing confidence that I could reach any goal that I set my mind to accomplishing. Somehow, the input of my eternally positive father, the excitement of my brother, whose opinion and approval I craved, and now with the endorsement of my college coach, I started to think beyond the satisfaction of preparing to compete and achieve my own elevated level of personal fitness. I started to contemplate winning. I dared to envision myself as a National Champion.

12

All my plans had succeeded beyond my expectations.

Results of *Step 1*: **The Food Plan**, included a total commitment to eating healthy foods and maintaining the minimal portion sizes needed to remain healthy enough to perform my job, my family obligations and my workouts. Maybe I overdid the food plan in the minimal lunches I ate, but I knew my body and I knew the depths of my limitations. I had completely changed my mindset about eating and revolved all consumption around need, rather than desire.

I had successfully executed *Step 2*: **The Measurement Plan**, maintaining meticulous records of my weight each day including how many miles I ran, my average monthly weight, my average weight loss month over month, my average daily mileage and my total average monthly mileage. I had goals of running 60 miles per month including an average of 7.5 miles or more per run and conducting more than 1,000 push-ups per week. I tracked all of this in a spreadsheet and logged data every day with graphs and charts to quickly show my trends and my progress against the goals I had set for myself.

I had become nearly perfect at understanding how each ounce of food affected my weight and how each unit of physical effort and exertion impacted my calorie burndown. I could stand on the scale at any hour of the day and predict within two tenths of a pound what I would weigh.

I had not backed down from *Step 3*: **The Exercise Plan**, hitting all the expected targets from the measurement plan and continuing to push myself beyond expectations. I even ran in another road race in the early Fall, coming in 14th place out of 750 competitors, averaging 6:30 minute miles and again, finishing fourth in my age division.

Additionally, *Step 4*: **The Disclosure Plan** was in full gear with my dad's attendance of my first tournament and my communications with Jay Jones and Rusty Carlsten. I also posted articles about my exploits on LinkedIn, which garnered nearly a thousand "Likes" and a couple hundred positive comments. The post also received numerous shares from people I knew from high school, college, various jobs and throughout my professional affiliations.

And, surprising myself, I had quite a robust <u>Step 5</u>: **The Strength Plan** going between my couple hundred pushups and sit-ups every few days and my sporadic trips to the gym to conduct curls, bench presses and other weight training to strengthen my glaring upper body deficiencies. During business conferences where I had to travel and stay in hotels, I sought the on-site gym and started running intervals to further develop my running speed. I'd run a quarter mile at a 7:30 pace and then notch the pace down by 15 seconds every half mile thereafter, challenging myself to see what combination of miles and pace I could reach. By the one-mile mark, I'd be down to 7:00. By the two-mile mark, I'd be at 6:30 and by three miles, I'd find myself sprinting a 5:45 mile. The best I accomplished was four miles with the last two quarters holding at 5:30.

I also took up skipping rope and found I could complete 2,000 jumps in increments of 500, which I felt would increase my footspeed and agility.

At a major technology conference in October that attracts more than 180,000 attendees in downtown San Francisco, I worked out like a madman in the hotel gym every night until midnight. I had the honor of presenting my expertise on a topic called "Overwhelming Benefit" on one of the keynote stages, appearing before tens of thousands of audience members. I also appeared on their closed caption television program, which they broadcast across the internet to their hundreds of thousands of customers and prospects worldwide. I looked back at the recording and loved how trim I looked in my slim fit khaki's and European cut jacket. The dents in either side of my face cast shadows where my cheeks used to bloat outward. And, with my nicely cut short hair, I looked back at myself and thought I was starting to look like the rugged, elite athlete I aspired to be. I also appeared 20 years younger and if I looked quickly, I saw the old college wrestler in my own sculpted face and especially in my eyes.

But, I needed a job. I had until the end of the year to find a new one. A few weeks before I learned of the potential shake-up at the Ad Tech firm, I had received a call from a recruiter about a company a few stops further down the subway line that needed someone of my experience and expertise for a Vice President role managing a much bigger team than the one I oversaw at the Ad Tech firm. Having only accrued a year and a half at the Ad Tech, and – at the time – not knowing anything about a possible layoff, I delayed my response.

But now, in need of a landing, I called them back and they invited me for a round of interviews. These interviews spanned a couple weeks and I ended up speaking to nearly a dozen different employees including several of the C-Suite executives. In the final interview, the hiring manager for the position, the SVP of Global Sales, sat across from me and asked me his opening question.

"Tell me how you can deliver '*Overwhelming Benefit*' here at our company," he asked.

I looked at him in surprise and he quickly revealed to me that one of his employees had heard me speak at the conference in San Francisco and he later Googled the video and watched it. He expressed how impressed he was in the content of my message and my influential presenting style. We launched into a productive discussion about the role and my qualifications to lead the team.

They offered me the job a week later. I had hurdled one more potential roadblock. This was a major relief as a prolonged, stressed-out job search would have crimped my ability to stay focused on my fitness, endurance and wrestling goals.

Of course, with starting a new job, I faced a new set of challenges. I had a bigger team, a much larger budget an enormous game-changing project to lead and scope of work that exceeded any challenge I had previously taken on in my career. The commute extended another 15 minutes longer and half my team lived on the west coast, in London or in Asia, which meant I would work much longer days. Fitting in my late-night workouts would not be easy. I'd have to intensify my resolve and heighten my focus on finishing my work, engaging in as much family time as I could and clinging to the successful routine I had established with all my might.

As the year flipped from 2016 to 2017 and the Nationals were set to take place "this year" rather than "next year", I faced the reality that I had to escalate my efforts to achieve Step 6: **The Work Out Plan**.

The two tournaments I wrestled were a good start. I obtained live wrestling experience and proved that I still had a place competing on the mat. But they only accounted for five individual matches, making up about 20-30 minutes of actual wrestling time. I needed more and I needed to practice actual moves.

I also had to clear the Workout Plan at home as it would entail leaving the house for an entire evening, driving to a faraway location, practicing for a couple hours and then driving home late at night. In a normal time, this activity would disrupt our family routine, but during the college application process and my wife's health struggles, it seemed like a non-starter.

By late November, my wife had agreed to another cortisone shot, this time with one of the preeminent New York hospitals in the country. And, for the most part, the treatment seemed to work. She felt much better. The numbness down her leg and into her foot dissipated soon after receiving the shot and her back pain dulled considerably. She slept through the night almost immediately for the first time in nearly a half of a year. Her mind cleared and her beautiful smile lit the walls of our home once again.

She had slept soundly for several weeks after the treatment, and didn't even wake up when I came in and out from running at night.

I tentatively asked her if I could participate in a couple wrestling practices and without hesitation, she said "yes".

"I'm fine now," she said with a genuine smile. "Go ahead and do what you need to do."

I started at the high school level, visiting Avon High School, my alma mater, where my brother, John, served as the head coach. He allowed me to practice with his team and

I spent two hours drilling moves, doing push-ups and sit-ups, running sprints and wrestling live with his 160 and 170 pounders.

At a shade over 140, the kids closer to my weight did not offer enough competition. And even after a few rounds of scrapping with his bigger guys, I still needed a challenge. So, I picked out the largest, most athletic looking kid in the room and asked him to wrestle against me. This kid turned out to be the 180-pound team captain who had a state ranking.

With him, I met my match. None of my moves worked on him as he was just too big and strong to beat. At one point, he slammed me face first into the mat and scuffed up my face. But I loved the beating and survived the practice with less stiffness in my neck than I had after the last tournament. The lifting weights had firmed up my core, neck and back. I could feel myself toughening up. I felt ready for the next challenge – my old college team.

Jay Jones invited me to practice with his squad on a Friday evening in Providence. I'd have to take a half day off from work and drive up before rush hour. As a bonus, they had practice on Friday evening and again on Saturday morning. I could drive up, workout for two hours, sleep over my dad's house about ten minutes away and then participate in a second workout the next morning.

I left myself the option to bail out on the second day if I took too much abuse during the first and didn't feel up to the second practice. But, honestly, I'd have to break a bone to stay away from that second workout.

There I stood, 48-years-old, facing 20 kids in their late teens and early 20s. They were in the prime of their lives, strong, fast and not particularly interested in getting beat by an old man like me. Jay slung his arm over my shoulder and introduced me. He pointed at my name on the wall where all the school's New England Champions are listed. And he asked me to say a few words before the practice started.

I told them that while I had won the New England championship in my senior year, during my junior year and every year leading up to my senior year, I wasn't good enough to make the team. I had better, faster, stronger wrestlers ahead of me and I just had to come to practice every day, run the miles, do the push-ups and sit-ups, drill the moves and take my beatings without the gratification of showing what I could do as a starter.

I asked them if they had goals and they all did. Most of their goals were what I would call outcome-oriented goals. They wanted to win a championship, place in the Nationals or just win some number of matches. Some of them just hoped to make the team. I revealed to them what my goal throughout college was, and they were surprised to learn that it was not to make the team, to win matches or to win a championship.

I told them that for three years, my goal was to wake up each morning, make it to every practice first and to be the hardest worker in the room. This was not a goal with a tangible reward. This was my daily objective and my supreme focus during every practice. I would look around the room, observe anyone who might be working harder than me and then double my efforts to outwork them. I figured that on a daily basis, I couldn't control whether I made the starting line-up. But I could control my own actions and how hard I worked. I had faith that it would pay off at some point. And at the tail end of my college career, it did. Eventually, I formed more specific goals to make the starting line-up and to win the championship. But it all started with the set of daily objectives to be the hardest worker in the room every day.

Today, as a business professional, I can face a room full of executives and present to them with confidence and self-assurance. But working out with those kids at full college-level intensity for two straight days; that was intimidating. At least, it was at first. It helped that my name hung on the banner over the practice room. It helped that they showed such respect for my past accomplishment. And it certainly helped that, as it turns out, I was relatively competitive in wrestling against them.

I felt rusty in my technique and Jay quietly pointed out gaps in my form, suggesting ways to improve my technique. In the live wrestling portion of the practice, I faced the 141-pound wrestlers. As it turned out, I had gotten down to 139 and they all ranged closer to 145 or 146. Possibly, I might have been better served facing the 133 pounders who all weighed about 136-137.

Regardless, I battled the 141 pounders well. I don't think I would have made the team or even the third string. But at one point, I tied up with one of the bigger 141 pounders, who weighed closer to 150 at the time. I felt him push into me. I felt his hips slide just off balance. I had his arms tied up just right. And without hesitation, I threw my hips into him, arched my back and pulled him right on top of my chest as I flew backward toward the mat with his weight born directly on my sternum. Just before crashing to the mat, I flexed my chest and turned my hips to flip him over my head and flat on his back. I had executed an impressive throw called a Lateral Drop, which would have amounted to a five-point move and a chance for a pin in a real match.

The other wrestlers including the assistant coach all cheered me for hitting the move. The wrestler I threw, impressed but unamused and somewhat embarrassed, quickly arched off his back. I grabbed his leg to hold on until the end of the period. To save face, he immediately tried to work a pinning move on me called a Spladle, which would punish me by splitting my legs apart in a painful stretch. I fought it off the best I could, but I knew I couldn't stop him. Mercifully, the assistant coach blew the whistle a few seconds early to put me out of my misery before suffering too much in the Spladle. It was all in fair competition and neither I nor my opponent had hard feelings about having scored the moves we did. I got the better of the adulation as his teammates jeered him for falling prey to my Lateral Drop and scoffed at him when he pointed out the Spladle that he had executed against me.

I realized that I had nothing but upside in wrestling against the kids. If I won, I was a hero. And if I lost, well, I was supposed to lose anyway.

I had a wonderful evening with my dad and slept relatively pain free in his comfortable spare bedroom. The next morning, I returned to practice at RIC. The team welcomed me back with smiles, pats on the back and high fives. I had earned their respect and they showed their appreciation for my contribution to their practice.

As part of my opening comments the day before, I had foolishly told them that I would challenge myself to be the hardest worker in their wrestling room over the course of the two days that I would spend practicing with them. It was another example of disclosing my objectives for the purpose of prodding myself to maintain my resolve and seek their encouragement along the way.

The most gratifying moment of the two-day experience came toward the end of the second practice. We were running sprints and I was starting to fade. I hung my head, slumped my shoulders and fell behind the other wrestlers in the room. The big 190-pound captain of the team came up behind me and quietly spoke into my ear for only me to hear.

"Hardest worker in the room – right coach?"

He totally understood. And his seven quick words motivated me to gut through the rest of the practice with my head held high. To this day, when I feel myself losing steam or my energy drop, I think of his words.

"Hardest worker in the room – right coach?"

And I find another level of strength to pick myself up. If I gained nothing else from the workout at RIC, I had that to carry with me into the National Championship tournament.

After showering in the coaches' locker room, I threw on a T-shirt and shorts and visited the team locker room. The wrestlers were sprawled out talking about girls, movies, classes and food. They all weighed themselves and changed into their street clothes. They asked me about my experience in college and what it was like to wrestle in the NCAAs. They asked me how I had managed to come down from 200 pounds. And they wished me luck in my training plan for the senior nationals.

I stepped onto the scale. The numbers on the digital screen flittered and settled on a number.

I weighed 137.4 pounds. Not only had I lost a total of 66 pounds since the start of the year, I had made weight for the Nationals. With three months to go, I was a pound and a quarter under.

Or, was I down to just 10 pounds over the next lower weight class of 127.75?

13

Starting sometime in May or June, 2016 when confidence that I could realistically compete in the USA Wrestling Nationals started to soar, I looked ahead at the calendar and identified two roadblocks that could hinder my success.

I had hit the road every other day or so and reached a great rhythm of running late at night after the family hit the sheets. But would I be able to continue the momentum come December, January and February in the bitter cold? Would a five-mile run in 0-degree weather with the arctic wind chill, five-foot snow dunes and black ice shut me into the house and block me from maintaining my momentum?

I had just successfully hit 137-pounds. I had made weight six weeks in advance, I had the luxury of settling in to the weight class and entering the tournament feeling completely at ease as a 138-pounder. I worried that I'd spend all that time and effort to lose the weight and gain great fitness only to give it all back to the blistering cold winter.

I also identified our nine-day family vacation to Disney World as a red flag. Sugary pancake and pastry breakfasts, fast food lunches and fancy dinners at sit down restaurants, night in and night out would surely obliterate the progress I had made with my weight, and fitness. Where would I run? Would I squeeze in my push-ups and sit-ups between the two Queen sized beds that my family of four would share for more than a week. I figured that nine vacation days could amount to at least a +10 on the scale, if not 15 or even more.

It wouldn't be so bad if it weren't jammed up in the year only about six weeks away from the Nationals. The timing stunk. Overcoming the 10-15 pounds I expected to pack on in that timeframe would come at the worst possible time. With my work commitments and the pressure of delivering my project, the cold northeast winter and the ticking clock, I dreaded what should have been the highlight of my year.

But instead of imagining bustling mornings on roller-coasters and carefree evenings in shorts and a t-shirt under the bright lights of the Disney fireworks, I pictured myself going off the rails and losing the discipline I had worked so hard to achieve.

I didn't want to come down to crunch time, the week of the tournament, still overweight and find myself trying to dehydrate on the four-hour flight to Iowa or sprinting through the corn fields to drip enough sweat to make weight. And I certainly didn't want to have to throw on the old plastics and drag the exercise bike into the steam room. I'm just too old for those shenanigans.

I had envisioned a nice leisurely flight. I pictured myself napping away without the stress of wondering what I weighed and how many tenths of a pound I might float between the 7am flight and the 5pm tournament weigh-in. I had hoped to leave Connecticut at 137-flat and not worry about getting to the UNI Dome with any danger of blowing the weigh-in.

The cold didn't turn out to bother me. I just bundled myself in a thin pajama bottom and thick sweat pants along with a thin cotton t-shirt, with a thicker long sleeve cotton t-shirt, a hooded sweat shirt and a plastic wind breaker. I threw on my favorite knitted cap and ski gloves and barely felt the cold air or the frozen wind chill. In fact, the reduced temperature made my body work harder to stay warm while the cold air energized my lungs. I found myself running as often in January as I had in July. I also took that turn at the top of the avenue and committed to the full ten-mile run down under the highway and all along the shore.

In fact, once I ran the 10-miler once, I made it a habit and started completing the route sometimes twice a week. I racked up nearly 200 miles between the months of December and February.

Disney turned out to present a greater challenge. For one, I had less leeway to decide when I wanted to eat and when I wanted to skip meals. In the office, away from the watching eyes of my wife and kids, I could snack on carrots for lunch. I could have an apple and some low sodium Wheat Thins. Or I could just all out skip lunch and wait until dinner time.

At home, I tried to keep up the impression that I had not made too many drastic changes to my eating patterns, other than reducing my meal sizes. I didn't want them to know the full scope of my approach.

Throughout the several weeks prior to the Disney trip, I had cut my breakfast intake to a handful of Life cereal or granola in the morning before I caught the train. During the work day, I engaged myself so intently in my work, that I plowed right through lunchtime without a scrap or even so much as a glass of water. I ate a little more at dinner where I made up for the depravity that I put myself through during the day. Nutritionists would tell you to do it the opposite way. Eat more in the morning and cut back in the evening. But I didn't want my family to see me eating scraps. I didn't want them to observe me engage in behavior that they would undoubtedly perceive to be unhealthy.

I generally knew what I was doing and when I needed nourishment. As well as I understood my caloric intake and the impact each mile had on my weight, I knew my body. I knew when I needed the vitamins in green vegetables, when I needed protein and when I needed a bit of dairy. I drank enough water to stay hydrated and regularly monitored the color of my pee every day.

I knew the tightness in my stomach every afternoon after consuming less than 4 ounces of nourishment was not perfectly healthy, but I also understood the bare minimum I needed to keep a healthy energy level and avoid malnourishment. I pushed that limit and played up to that line. But I took care of myself in a way I knew would work for me.

I also knew my family would not understand. And I'm sure doctors and nutritionists would point out how risky my behavior was. But that was the whole point. It wasn't unhealthy behavior. It was just risky. I felt like I had total control over my body and knew what I needed and when I needed it. I had done it before in high school and college. I had the experience to toe that line and the motivation to stick with it.

However, in Disney, we spent every waking hour together as a family. I had much less control of my schedule and no time to myself to make my own choices. We ate where and when the kids wanted to eat, which left me little choice in an environment filled with minimal options for low calorie, high energy health-conscious meal selection. When the family grabbed burgers and fries at the snack shop, I wasn't going to skip an entire meal and allow them to see me sit there with nothing to eat. I'd select whatever I could find that fit my Food Plan; a wilted salad, a chicken sandwich on a bleached white role, a rice bowl with some sort of pork-like meat.

I managed to escape breakfast time with a handful of granola each morning. Occasionally, I'd finish my wife's half eaten croissant or take a bite or two of a cinnamon bun that one of my boys left on their plates. The dinners gave me the most difficult challenges. It's not like any of the menu selections presented two ounces of meat with four ounces of vegetables. And I didn't want to leave so much on my plate each night to cause the family alarm bells that dad is starving himself.

Plus, I must admit, all the food looked so good, I just couldn't stop taking that one last bite over and over again. In the lobby of our hotel every night, a spread of amazing deserts; key lime pies, pecan pies, cheese cakes, cupcakes with mounds of frosting, chocolate chip and sugar cookies all sat out on display, free for the taking.

They lined the trays in bite-sized portions with spotlights shining down on them. And I just couldn't lay off. I found the more I ate, the hungrier I grew and the more I could rationalize that one more two-ounce key lime desert wouldn't make that big of a difference.

They tasted so delightful. I experienced a burst of joy every time I ingested one of the tiny little treats. The heavenly combination of sweet crust and gooey sugar lit up my taste buds. And the portions were so small, I found it too easy to rationalize each transgression.

So, where I had previously been relegating breakfast to a handful of granola completely skipping lunch during the week days and cutting my dinners to about the amount of food that could fit in the palm of my hand, I was now eating at least double the amount of breakfast, closer to a full lunch, definite full-sized dinners and numerous high calorie sugar deserts every night.

It felt weird, although perversely nice at the same time, to walk around the parks with a full stomach. I hadn't eaten like that in at least six months. But I also knew that I was starting to realize my worst fears.

I don't know why it didn't occur to me until a few days into the vacation, but I asked the concierge if they had a workout room on the hotel property. I just never equated Disney with working out. When you go to a Marriott in Dallas, Texas, you expect a workout room. But at the Grand Floridian Hotel, it just didn't seem like a necessary amenity. Who goes to Disney and works out?

Apparently, someone does because, as it turns out, they did have a small gym on site. It had a couple treadmills, one or two nautilus machines and a rack of free weights.

So, one night, about halfway into the trip, I asked my wife if she would mind if I went to work out after she and the boys fell asleep for the evening. They were all so tired from walking the parks all day, they typically dropped off into deep slumber around 9pm. My wife had no problem with it if I returned quietly and showered before I came to bed.

That night, I waited until everyone dozed off, threw on my running shoes and a pair of shorts with one of my t-shirts and headed off to the gym. The clock showed about 9:45pm. The first item I looked for was a scale and thankfully they had the same metal scale as my doctor in the corner of the room. Before leaving for Disney, I had reached 137 pounds and held that line for a week. Now, I stepped on the scale. I fearfully predicted 150 and begged God not to make me move the large counter weight from the 100 mark to the 150 mark. If I weighed any more than 150, I'd kick myself for falling off the rails so badly.

I registered about 146. That wasn't so bad. I had gained close to 10 pounds. I had a month and a half until the Nationals. I felt like I could manage that.

Another guy, a younger dude, entered the room as I started up the treadmill. One phenomenon I discovered was that with ten extra pounds of food in my stomach, I had an extra bit of pep and energy. I started off running a half mile at a 7:30 minute pace. But quickly felt like running faster. So, each half mile, I notched the pace down by 30 seconds. I ran the second half mile at seven minutes and the third half at 6:30. By the third mile, I found myself all out sprinting at a five-minute pace.

I hadn't run in more than a week. But I felt amazingly strong and fit.

After banging out 200 push-ups and sit ups in four groups of 50, I curled the free weights, did some fly-ups and a few other strength exercises. Occasionally, I nodded in a friendly way to the 20-something guy who shared the room with me.

Then I saw the rack of jump ropes. In high school, I loved emulating Rocky Balboa with the jump rope. I taught myself to sling the rope with lightning speed and then cross my arms and then whip the jump rope through the air twice beneath each jump. I didn't know if I could still skip rope as well, but decided to give it a try.

It turns out that jumping rope is a lot like riding a bike. The skill stays with you many years later. So, I grabbed that rope, stared at myself in the mirror and ripped off 1,000 hops. It took me about ten minutes. The rope whistled as it sliced through the air. My running shoes barely made a sound as the pads of my feet bounced gingerly above the rope – leaving just the half inch clearance needed for it to swing through, loop over my head and snap back through again.

Sweat poured down my stone face as I stared almost catatonically into the mirror. And when I finished, I felt so good, that I went back to the treadmill and ran two more miles at a six-minute pace. And when I finished the two-mile sprint, with the clock reading 11:15pm, I grabbed the jump rope again and banged out another 1,000 hops. By 11:25, the younger muscular guy left the room. As he did, I could see him look back over his shoulder with a twisted expression of shock and admiration for my insane workout. I wanted to make it a clean 11:30, so I plowed out 500 more jumps.

I stripped off my soaked t-shirt, peeled back my slimy socks and hit the scale. I had lost 3 and a half pounds and weighed a manageable 142.5. I was down to only a five-pound weight gain from my average the week prior.

I skulked back into the room, took a shower and laid in bed. I could feel the blood run through my veins. My stomach already felt like it had streamlined from the slight bulge I felt before the workout. I slept like a baby and woke up the next morning with the most amazing energy I had felt in a long time.

I realized the benefit of eating more and then converting it to energy through my workouts.

I hit that gym for at least an hour and a half every night for the next five nights. I ran insanely fast miles, averaging below a six-minute pace for three, four, sometimes five miles at a clip. I worked my push-up and sit-up count to 250 and jumped rope 2,500, 3,000 and eventually 5,000 times one night.

I didn't change my eating habits during the vacation, but with the extreme workouts, my weight stabilized right around 140.

By the time we arrived home and I hit the little scale in our upstairs bathroom, I registered at a perfectly acceptable 139.6. The vacation had not hurt me at all. In fact, it taught me a few lessons. For one, I could eat more and still stay on track. For two, I could run much faster than I even believed, and I could sustain a pace that would win local road races for many miles at a time. And for three, I felt like Rocky Balboa in my ability to workout with such passion and focus.

Where I expected the family vacation to set me back, I had succeeded in moving another step forward in my crazy Headlock plan to carve myself back into the athlete I had been in college. I was getting there. I could feel it.

With the weather turning slightly for the better and the vacation behind me, I had no roadblocks left between me and the national championship which was now 45 days away.

14

The USA Wrestling website advertised that registration for the Nationals would open on January 1st, 2017. I had bookmarked the site and watched it daily waiting for the greyed-out registration button to turn red.

First the site indicated that registration would open on January 1st. Then the tournament organizers delayed it until January 11th. A second delay pushed it out to January 14th. A message urged competitors to register quickly before they filled all their available slots and that only the first 1,500 registrants would be allowed to compete in the Masters division.

January 14th came and went and the registration site still did not activate. I sent e-mails and called the office, but they did not get back to me right away. I worried about getting wrapped up in my work, or in family activities and losing track of checking the web site every day. I would have kicked myself if I had come all this way only to miss the registration window. While that risk seemed low, I also wanted to make my flight and hotel arrangements and couldn't do so until I successfully completed the registration. The longer it took, the more expensive the flight and the less choice of arrival times I would have.

Finally, the button turned red and registration opened. I clicked it. I entered my credit card information and my USA Wrestling ID number. I received my confirmation by e-mail and then promptly handled my flight and hotel accommodations. After 12 months of hard work, the whole Headlock commitment had just turned vividly real. I was truly going to do this. I had a confirmation number, a travel itinerary, a hotel reservation code and a rental car waiting for me at the airport in Iowa. Twenty-six years after competing in the NCAAs in college, I was going to compete in the National Championship again, this time as a 48-year-old Master.

And this time, unlike my experience in college, I was not going to struggle to make weight. I was not going to think of the Nationals as an afterthought as I had in college where I was so obsessed with winning the New England Championship the week before, I had no emotional connection to the NCAAs.

I remember ballooning from 126 pounds at the New England tournament in college to 145 in less than three days. By the end of the weekend, I had gained almost 20 pounds. The extra heft probably helped me overpower my opponent in the finals. But it made the next week of preparing for the NCAAs hell.

Unfortunately, the strain of cutting those 20 pounds in four days robbed me of the appropriate mental preparedness I needed to compete at my best. I lost my first match to the wrestler who came in 8th place by the dreadful score of 14-1 in a wretched performance where I basically failed to compete at any level close to my ability.

I pulled myself together and wrestled well in my second match, but dropped a close one 10-6 to the competitor who ultimately came in 5th place.

Dejected from losing, with the realization that I had just wrestled in my last college wrestling match ever, I shuffled off the mat to find a quiet place to reflect. That was when they tapped me on the shoulder and told me they had picked me – the skinniest kid in the tournament – for a random drug test.

I couldn't get a sip of water. I couldn't change out of my sweaty clothes. I just had to walk straight to the bathroom and pee in a cup in front of an NCAA enforcement monitor.

In any case, my college career ended that day in defeat. The week prior, I had won the New England Championship with my hand raised to a chorus of cheers from my teammates, classmates, friends, family and a field house full of people I didn't even know. But at the NCAAs, having entered a few pounds over and forced to run wind sprints in a boiler room to make weight, I lost two straight in a lackluster performance, peed in a cup and then just wandered around in my street clothes for the next day as my teammates all wrestled in the championship rounds to earn the All-American status that I failed to acquire.

Twenty-six years later, as I found myself training for the Masters version of the National Championship, I often thought back to my college experience. Had I managed my weight more responsibly and not allowed it to cause such a distraction, would I have wrestled better? Would I have brought more focus and confidence with me into those matches? Could I have performed better? Was I good enough to have earned All-American honors?

I absolutely believe so.

And that's why I worked so hard to stabilize my weight over the long haul and take the whole "cutting weight" dynamic out of my competitive equation. As of March 1st, with exactly a month to go, I stabilized my weight between 136.6 and 138.6. I could eat my dry cereal for breakfast, manage a small, but solid lunch and eat well at dinner and remain in the target zone. The weight class of 138.75 would be a cinch if I didn't completely fall off a wagon and drastically change my patterns. I had my routine. I had a mere four weeks to go. I ran. I did my push-ups and sit-ups. I lifted. I had put it all together and was ready to go. Nothing could stop me.

I Googled past results of the USA Wrestling National Championships to gain a sneak peek at what the competition might resemble this year. In 2013, there had been five competitors at 138.75 pounds. I Googled each one. Most of them had wrestled at strong Division I schools in and around Iowa such as Minnesota, Wisconsin, Indiana, Purdue and UNI. Many of them coached at colleges or high schools and ran local wrestling clubs in their towns. I watched YouTube videos of the championship matches and instantly recognized that these competitors were all legitimate, strong, fast and talented. I could go there and compete, or I could get my doors blown off.

Despite seeing how strong the competition looked, I still had no idea what to expect of myself. On the one hand, I had barely wrestled in a quarter century. On the other hand, I was in the best shape of my life since my early 20s and I had performed reasonably well in a variety of competitive environments. I didn't let the YouTube videos sway my confidence one way or the other. But I recognized the bottom line that the caliber of competitor would be high at the tournament.

In 2015, there were only two wrestlers in the weight class and they wrestled each other in a best of three series. I reviewed the page that detailed the 2016 results and was dismayed to see that there were no entrants in the 138.75-pound weight class that year.

Around March 1st, the USA Wrestling website displayed a page with all the age divisions and weight classes arranged in a table. You could log in, look up your weight class and see how many other competitors you would face in the tournament. I scrolled over to my age group and weight class and was instantly distressed to see that there were no entrants in the 138.75 class this year. In fact, I was the only registrant in the entire age group.

I couldn't believe that I ran the risk of spending all year training for a tournament that would not attract any participants. I bookmarked the page and revisited the site every day to check. Registrations added up for the younger age brackets, but not in the Masters division.

I tried to put it out of my mind and stay on track in my regimen. At times, I allowed myself to lament *"what's the point?"*. I imagined everyone asking me how I did at the tournament and having to respond that I trained for a year, ran 600 miles, did 10,000 push-ups and starved myself to pick up a forfeit and a paper championship. I could picture my wife looking at me like I had wasted my time and money.

Part of me knew why the tournament had a low turnout. Folkstyle wrestling is less popular among college graduates as the focus turns to Freestyle, which is the style used in the Olympics. It seems that in past years, the turn-out were higher, but had trailed off more recently. I e-mailed the tournament director asking if he thought more people would sign-up and if I should cancel my flight arrangements while I still could. He didn't reply.

I kept the turnout issue to myself and proceeded full speed. I'd fly there no matter what and take the forfeit if I had to. A big part of my objective was to go through the journey and the preparation to compete. The resulting physical transformation would be the reward, regardless of any results I generated on the mat. The nature of the competition was not supposed to matter as much to me. I had set out to prove to myself that I could do everything right and get to Iowa ready to take on whomever showed up. But, now that I had exceeded all those goals, I wanted to compete. I wanted to win. I just hoped someone would show up.

My wife, who had grown more supportive and almost excited for me over the months since her back started to feel better suggested that I ask my dad to come with me to the tournament. I could see her thinking that she would not want to travel alone if she were in my shoes and assumed I would be lonely flying out there myself.

A big part of me wanted to invite him. Another part of me wanted to ride out there totally on my own, lost in my own thoughts and processes. I wasn't sure I wanted to have to interact with another person, even my dad, who I adore more than almost anyone else in the world.

Plus, and I hated to think this, but he had grown older. He wouldn't move through the airport as quickly as me. He had his routines in the morning. I wondered if it would be distracting to have a companion. I wondered if he would have the stamina to sit in the bleachers all day waiting for my matches. As a 50-year-old dad, he handled it all like a trouper. Pushing 80, I worried about him.

I thought back to my high school and college years. My dad had always been my number one fan. He showed up at every match with his video camera and diligently filmed every minute including the ensuing hugs from my coaches, high fives with my teammates and celebrations with my classmates. I have all those tapes in a box. I converted some of them to digital and still watch them every few years with great nostalgia and pride.

I only learned to appreciate his efforts once I became a father myself and started filming my own boys with my digital video camera at their sports events. I have since realized the sacrifice he made as you can't watch the game or competition and enjoy it when you are chained to the camera and have to focus on framing the shot and following the action. My poor dad spent all those years with his eye crammed into the viewer of his camera and his neck torqued so that I could have these amazing memories on video.

I also thought about all those car rides back from matches and tournaments where he would recap his impressions of what I had done well and repeatedly congratulate me on my accomplishments. How could I even consider not inviting him to join me in Iowa? As an adult, with my own family, I struggled to set aside time to spend with him. When I did see him, it was typically at a family party or gathering with dozens of other people. And here I had this golden opportunity to spend a weekend with him in a one-on-one setting and I balked?

I decided I wanted to share the experience with him. But I continued to hesitate. I felt almost embarrassed that nobody had signed up for the tournament and even wondered if they would cancel it.

The director assured me in an e-mail several days after I reached out to him, that others would register. But as of three weeks out, I was still the only one at any weight class in my age division.

A 152-pounder popped up in the Masters Class A division, which consisted of 25 to 32-year-olds. I considered asking if I could compete in that class if I had to. It would be quite a challenge to wrestle Division I recent graduates in a weight class 15 pounds heavier than my current frame while giving up 20 years of youth. But I had overcome so many other challenges, I just took this one in stride and adjusted my expectations to adapt to the situation.

I continued to check the site daily. I made a note to call my dad, but kept hesitating, hoping another 138-pounder would show up in the 45 to 52-year-old division. I had hoped to compete against more than one other. But if it came down to a best of three wrestle off with one wrestler in my weight class, I'd take that. At least I'd earn the medal or trophy or whatever you get for winning as opposed to accepting an honor simply for showing up.

Then with about two and a half weeks to go, a new registrant appeared next to the 127.75-pound weight class. I was still the only 138-pounder. But there was now someone signed up for the next weight class below me. I stared at the number "1" next to the row for the 127-pound class. I wondered if the 127-pounder would consider wrestling up at 138, just as I had contemplated going up to the 152-pound class in the A Division.

And then, the simple answer hit me. I had to wrestle at 127-pounds. That would guarantee that I'd have at least one competitor to face. If I was going to win the National Championship, I wanted to do it on the mat. I wanted to beat someone for the honor and not just earn it for showing up.

In thinking it through more deeply, the reality hit me. I had already lost 65 pounds. My frame had almost no fat left. My third round of pants, mostly 31-inch -waist, were falling off. I spent most of my days with a completely empty stomach. I could hear gurgling and rumbling on a regular basis.

I thought making 138 would mark the end of my weight loss journey. But I was wrong. I stared at the website and the roster of registered competitors and made the decision. I locked it into my head, making another Headlock pact with myself. Part of me feared what would come next. Part of me found the synergy of returning to my college weight class of 126 pounds as a poetic bookend to my wrestling career. The biggest part of me just shrugged off any concerns and moved forward as I typically do, when faced with a nearly insurmountable challenge. Once the goal locked into my mind, I would not be able to back off it.

I had to lose ten more pounds to get to 127 and I had two and half weeks to do it.

15

During my journey from a rotund 201-pound middle aged dad, to whatever I had become at my new gaunt 137 iteration, my boys transitioned from admiring my efforts, to worrying about my well-being.

"You're too skinny," they'd say. *"Why don't you bulk up and wrestle at a higher weight class?"*

Many people asked me that question during my high school and college years. The answer is not as simple as most people might think. And, to be honest, I don't know that my answer is a universal truth. In my experience and among the majority wrestlers from my era, the prevailing opinion was that slimming down to the lowest possible weight class is the better way to optimize your competitive advantage than "bulking up", especially among lightweights like I was in the 1980s and 90s.

The ideal scenario entailed cutting any excess fat, trimming down to the lowest achievable weight class while simultaneously building as much strength as possible. During my freshman year of college, wrestling at 118 pounds at Central Connecticut State University, the head trainer determined my body fat percentage at 4.7%, far below average even for highly active athletes. While I didn't "bulk-up", I did conduct the push-up and sit-up ladder every practice. I ran a good 3-4 miles per day and I wrestled in the room, utilizing every available muscle in my body. I believe the combination of elevated strength and reduced body fat that I achieved at that time represented the best possible athletic mix.

Could I have "bulked up" a weight class or two – say to 142? Well, first, I would not have made the Rhode Island College starting line-up at 142 as we had a two-time New England Champion who earned All-American honors at that weight class during my senior year. I couldn't have made the team at 134 either because of our four-time New England Champ who was a two-time All American at that weight class. They were two of the three reasons why I never made the team until my senior year when the opening popped up at 126.

But setting that aside, no matter how strong I became as a natural 150-pound guy, wrestling in the 142-pound weight class, I would have run into numerous other bigger competitors who cut down from 170 or higher, and who already had a bigger base of "bulk" than me. They would have made it to 142 by trimming their body fat like I had while also retaining the majority of their greater strength. In other words, there are two ways to optimize your Body-Mass Index; increase muscle or decrease fat. The ultimate is to do both at the same time.

Since I wrestled in college, new philosophies and approaches have arisen as well as quite appropriate concerns about the health and safety of high school wrestlers. Most high school athletic commissions across the country have set new rules to disallow the extreme weight loss associated with the sport, which has made the "bulking up" strategy more attractive than it used to be.

But I had to approach this objective the only way I knew how. Right or wrong, I had to conduct myself in my own way.

"The boys are confused," my wife told me one night, lying in bed next to me. "You don't look like the dad they grew up with. They're worried you're going to have a heart attack or get injured. You're so skinny. You think you look great, because this is what you looked like in college and when we met. But when they look at you, they don't necessarily see how you've built up your neck and back, or how your chest and biceps might be a little stronger. They see your sunken cheeks, your hollow eyes and your ribs sticking out on either side of your stomach. And they just think you look sick."

It hurt to hear the feedback. I hadn't looked at this from their perspective in quite that way. It bothered me to think I had created confusion or anxiety in their minds.

"Why are you doing this?" she asked me. "I get that you are doing it for your own reasons and I know you well enough that there will be no stopping you. But, do you really know why it has become so important to you?"

I thought about her question. I tried to answer it. I didn't have much of an answer. I thought about quoting George Mallory, the first person to climb Mount Everest and say; *"Because it's there."* But I thought I should give my wife a little more perspective than that obscure quote that popped into my head.

"Honestly, I don't know exactly why," I said to her as I stared at the darkened bedroom ceiling. "I just feel compelled to accomplish something; something great; something exceptional. You only get so many skills and abilities in life that truly set you apart from everybody else. They're like your God-given gifts in life. I guess I just wanted to see how far I could push myself. I wanted to expand beyond my limits.

And I wanted to maximize what I accomplished with my gifts."

"Why now?" she asked. "You could have done this 25 years ago when you were still in your 20s, before we had the family. It would have been much easier for you."

I thought about that, but I knew that answer.

"In my 20s, I had to work so hard to get my career off the ground," I replied. "I was a Creative Writing Major and not at any sort of Ivy League college by any stretch. I started at a very low salary and worked insanely long hours to make my way up the ladder. I worked past midnight on a regular basis to accelerate my career. And my approach succeeded very well. But it didn't lend itself to training for a national wrestling tournament. Plus, I had just spent 10 years killing myself for the sport. I needed a break. Then the kids came, and we wrapped ourselves around their activities and the years just flew by. I spent so much of my time coaching their sports, running their leagues and serving on the boards of those organizations, I had no time left to myself."

"I get that," she replied, almost wistfully. "I understand wanting to do something for yourself."

"I feel so much better about myself since I gave up television, started eating healthy foods and filling my time with more productive activities like working out and writing," I continued. "For so many years, I worked, I organized the kids' sports teams, I put in the time coaching, I dealt with all the ridiculous parents and the politics of the programs. And at the end of each night, I was so mentally worn out, that I just plopped on the couch, flipped the channels and gorged on ice cream. It feels so much better to wake up every morning and decide to make every moment of the day productive."

"That's good," she replied.

"Why am I doing this?" I reiterated her initial question. "I don't know specifically why. I just know that I feel compelled to do it. And, like you said, I can't stop until I see it through to the end."

It was March 13th. I had just under three weeks to go.

"It will all be over soon," I assured my wife.

But I knew I would never be the same. I was too motivated to convert whatever gifts of talent I had to accomplishments. I would keep wrestling in local tournaments and seek to return to the nationals the next year and possibly every year after for the foreseeable future. I'd also continue running in road races, looking to start winning – and not just in my age group. I wanted to win outright against all the ages.

At the beginning of February, I had pushed my mileage to 10. And, once I ran 10 miles, I couldn't go back to any amount less than that. I started running 10 miles every time I left the house to workout. While it took a few days to recover, I found myself able to run the 10-spot about twice a week. I ran close to 70 miles in February – even with the 9 days in Disney injected into that month.

During the first two weeks of March, I continued the pattern. But a new thought that had simmered in my mind emerged. I could take a right turn at the church at the last intersection and add a three-mile loop to the 10-mile course. That would equate to a half marathon.

The national championship took place on April 1st. The following weekend, on April 9th, I had seen an advertisement for a half-marathon competition. I decided I would enter the race when I returned from Iowa. I had run 10 miles nearly a dozen times over the past 45 days. I could suffer through three more.

I left the house on March 13th. I weighed 137 on the dot. I felt strong on my feet and well rested. I had taken off more time between runs than usual due to family obligations each night. As I set off to run my 10 miles, I dreaded the work and sacrifice it would take to make it to the 127-pound weight class.

I figured I'd have to weigh about 128 ½ by the time I left for Iowa and that I could float the remaining ¾ pounds to get to 58 Kilograms, which was the precise measurement I had to hit. I wasn't sure I could count on the float as I'd be at rock bottom in the high 120s. My stomach would be completely empty, so my metabolism would slow down or even stop altogether.

This had happened to me numerous times in high school and college where I emptied my stomach so drastically for such an extended period that I could no longer count on my natural engine to burn off those last pounds. I had to rely on extreme short-term dehydration to lose the last pound or two, which often made me feel sick and bereft of energy. I also found myself heaving up green bile – literally the color of anti-freeze.

I didn't want to find myself in that situation. At 48-years-old, winning a national championship, especially if the field consisted of only one competitor, just wasn't worth that amount of aggravation, physical risk and potential harm.

The few times this happened to me, I usually wrestled poorly. In my senior year of college, after having won a prestigious national-caliber pre-season tournament, I gained too much weight by generally making stupid, immature choices. I pigged out on pepperoni pizza, soda, cookies, massive brownie hot fudge sundaes and milkshakes. I had that brash overconfidence of youth and believed I could bound right back from bouncing up from 126 to 140 in three days. By the end of the week, I made it back to 126, but I was so sick at the weigh-in that by the time I stepped onto the mat for the opening home dual meet of the season, I had almost no energy.

My opponent, a Division II All-American from Saint Lawrence College, entered our building and blew my doors off. I barely put up a fight. He knocked me off my feet in front of all my classmates and manhandled me to the point of embarrassment. I lost 17-2.

One month later, having learned my lesson and managed my weight more responsibly, I wrestled the same competitor in a tournament at Worcester Polytechnic University and crushed him worse than he had beaten me, winning by pin after throwing him around the mat for two periods.

I took the lesson of that match forward into my journey as a 48-year-old and swore to myself that I would lose the weight gradually and with unwavering discipline to avoid the scenario where I compete below my best ability due to a negative reaction of losing too much weight too quickly.

Despite the lessons learned in my 20s, I found myself at 48-years-old facing a situation where I had 10 pounds to lose in 17 days after having already spent an entire year carefully crafting a path from 201 to 138. While I had averaged 8-10 pounds lost per month in the beginning of the year, throughout the back half of the year, I had stabilized in the low 140s and nudged downward by only a pound or two each month.

So, on that March 13th run, I engaged in two deep thought-processes. For one I planned how I would have to drop the 10 pounds to 127.75. I'd have to break from 137 to less than 135 that night and float to 134 by the morning. It was a Sunday night and I'd have to hold 134 through Friday, March 17th, when I could run another five miles and look to lose another pound and a half or two. That would put me at about 132.5 with exactly two weeks to go. I'd probably have to give back about a pound or two if I felt too weakened from the faster drop and the more extreme depletion of my stomach.

So, the following Wednesday, March 22nd I figured I could try to push myself into another ten-miler and try to get down just under 131, assuming I'd be coming from about 133 or 133.5. This would put me at three pounds over with just more than a week to go. I'd have to hold 131 or 132 at the most until the weekend before the tournament. That would be my last chance to run 10 more miles as I would not want to tire myself too close to the competition. I'd have to break 130 on that run and finish as close to 129 as possible. If I struggled to execute the plan and found myself still stuck in the 30s, I'd have to run one more time during the week before the tournament. But I wouldn't want to do too many more than 3-4 miles that close to the competition. If I could get to 129 by Wednesday, March, March 29th, I could manage my intake from there and drift toward 128.5 over the remaining few days before the Saturday morning flight to Iowa. I'd land at 1:00pm and the weigh-in would take place from 4pm-5pm. With the one-hour drive from the airport, that would leave me little time to throw on the plastics and suck out the last little bit if I were still overweight at that point.

Once I made weight, I'd have the evening to rehydrate, replenish my energy, eat as much as I could handle without overloading myself and get a solid night's sleep before the start of the competition at 9am the next morning. I'd have to choose foods that could provide valuable nutrients and high energy. But I'd need light foods that would not crash my stomach and overpower my digestive system. I'd also have to rehydrate slowly but steadily to avoid the vomiting reaction I had experienced in the past when I rehydrated too quickly.

As I mentioned, I had two thought-processes that evening on March 13th. In addition to planning my weight loss schedule from 137 to 127, I contemplated my running goals. I thought further about the half marathon after the nationals. I hadn't planned on it, but as I reached the end of my 10-mile route, I just turned right at the church instead of left and added the three-mile loop to complete the practice half-marathon. I ran with decent pace and finished in a total of 1 hour and 40 minutes, just under an eight-minute pace.

I decided to sign up for the half and work toward a full marathon by the end of the year.

That night, when I returned from my epic 13-miler, I showered, drank two ounces of water and stepped on the scale. Damn the plan, I weighed 133, nearly two less than expected.

I woke up the next morning at 132.4, almost two pounds less than the plan I had just made. And, I felt fine. I had energy. I peed a decent amount. The color had a healthy shade of yellow. I felt like I could navigate my day on the same minimal food and drink as usual.

I looked in the mirror at my image, obscured by the steam of the shower and pointed at myself with a huge self-satisfied grin.

"Not only did you just assure yourself of making 127," I told myself. "You just won yourself a National Championship."

16

My dad came down from Rhode Island and we stayed together in a hotel in town the night before our flight to Iowa. I weighed a manageable 129-pounds. I had completed my last five-mile run on Wednesday and felt amazingly strong, energetic and healthy.

Knowing that I would make 127 without having to rely on extreme measures, I was giddy to invite my dad to join me for the weekend. He ate with the family - although I had 4 ounces of pasta and nothing more - and we had a delightful evening shooting the breeze and connecting. My kids shared their stories about school and sports. My wife brightened our dining room with her charm and I just sat back enjoying the relaxed evening – a sort of calm before the storm.

In fact, weather reports of a storm started popping up a few days earlier with predictions of 8-10 inches of snow. I worried that my flight would be cancelled, and I'd miss the tournament altogether. But fortunately, the storm stayed far north of us and we only received a healthy dose of rain.

I awoke on Saturday morning, April 1st. I slept like a baby in the hotel. I had weighed out at 127.2, a half-pound under the weight class of 127.75 on the bathroom scale the previous night. So, I knew I had little concerns about making weight. But on principle, I decided that I would neither eat nor drink a morsel of food the entire day until we arrived in Iowa and I officially completed my weigh-in procedure.

My dad suggested I take a drink of water or a bite of an apple. But I refused. I didn't know how accurately my bathroom scale might match the official scale at the tournament and I didn't want to create any margin for error.

We arrived at the airport. Our flight listed on the board as "On Time", leaving at 11:40am and arriving in Iowa at 1:30pm, giving us three hours to make the one-hour drive to the 4:30pm registration. And then the delay notice appeared. A one-and-a-half-hour delay. Butterflies floated across my stomach at that point. I had worked so hard to avoid any stress associated with the logistics of getting to the weigh-in without issue. And now, I had to wonder if I'd be speeding across the Iowa highways just to make it in time.

Fortunately, we landed with two-and-a-half hours' leeway and we made it with 45 minutes to spare.

I stood waiting for them to open the weigh-in room. I gazed out across the University of Northern Iowa athletic dome, which stretched across the entire length of an indoor football stadium. Lined up one abutted against the other, were 22 separate wrestling mats. The glare from the overhead spotlights glinted off the shiny flat surfaces and made me squint.

My stomach tightened from my fast and I could feel little pills of skin curl and separate from my dried-out lips. I watched the clock, literally staring at it turn from 4:15 to 4:16, to 4:17 and on. Finally, at 4:20, they let me down into the room. I registered, stepped on the scale and took a deep breath as the official called out my weight to the tournament director.

"McLaughlin – 125.4" he said as he wrote my number on my shoulder with a permanent marker.

It's funny how miserable you can feel until you receive an emotional boost and then, without any change in your physical condition, experience a surge of energy. I packed my bag and sprinted up the staircase looking for the water fountain.

The culmination of 16 months spent so focused on my objective to compete in the nationals had finally come to fruition. I had embarked on a life-changing journey to employ a "Big Vision, a Bold Strategy and a Brave Approach". I had implemented six distinct plans including "01: The Food Plan", "02: The Exercise Plan", "03: The Strength Plan", "04: The Measurement Plan", "05: The Disclosure Plan" and "06: The Workout Plan". Resulting from these game-changing plans, I had run 650 miles, I trained myself to endure a half marathon, I conducted 10,000 push-ups and sit-ups and I had lost a grand total of 76 pounds from 201 to less than 126, my college weight class from 1991.

The thought even occurred to me that at 125.4, I was only 7 pounds heavier than my wife.

I looked forward to dinner with my dad that night. Traveling with him, spending one-on-one time together and discussing our family experiences, our family history, politics, religion, sports and even topics as mundane as the weather gave me great joy. Too often, when I see my dad, it's at a family function with dozens of other people. And even more often, the busy schedules and commitments I have with my own family make it difficult to set aside time to spend with him. He does a great job in understanding these constraints. But it still makes me sad that I don't see him more often.

But the ability to focus exclusively on him in Iowa; listen to him, share stories of my job and my family experiences; win or lose, sharing this event with him turned out to be one of the most wonderful outcomes of the entire journey.

In terms of eating my dinner, I knew I had to exercise restraint. I had to eat slowly and choose foods that would provide energy, hydration, a little protein and nutrients. I started with granola, just to fill my stomach with enough sustenance to quell my hunger and still provide a little energy. In the past, I had made the mistake of drinking too much water on an entirely empty stomach and suffering the flood of water spewing out the back end with no solid food anywhere in the digestive system to slow its mad rush. The granola provided a filter-like base to retain the water and enable my body to absorb more of it.

My second move was to find a grocery store and buy grapes. The natural sugar and high volume of juice in each little round ball of goodness would give me even more energy and continue to help me rehydrate.

I thought through what I wanted to eat for my meal and decided meatloaf would be a good choice. The beef would be a good source of protein, but in hamburger form and mingled with bread and egg, it would be a little easier on my stomach. I couldn't find a place that served meatloaf, so I had shepherd's pie. The combination of mashed potatoes for some carbohydrates, meat and vegetables turned out to be a great choice.

However, I made a fatal flaw. I enjoyed the oversized plate of food so much that I didn't stop when I should have. I ate about a third of the plate and told myself to put down the fork. But I didn't listen. I ate another third and begged myself to stop. And I did; at first. Then I decided to pick some of the vegetables out of the gravy. And then they brought me my side of asparagus. And the asparagus had been sautéed in butter, salt and ginger. It tasted so good, so I ate most of that. And I continued to drink big ice-cold glasses of water.

When I stood up from the table, my stomach ached. I thought I would throw up. I couldn't stand straight. Walking to the car hurt my stomach even more as my gait caused my insides to wobble back and forth.

When we arrived back at the hotel, I tried to go to the bathroom, but couldn't. It felt like the food had congregated high at the top of my stomach and bunched up in a sort of traffic jam. I knew this phenomenon well. Because I had cut back on my food intake for so long, my stomach had shrunk. The muscles along the lining of my stomach had contracted and stiffened to address the reduced throughput.

Then, when I consumed an abnormally high volume of food, there was not enough room in my stomach to store it all while my digestive acids broke it down and sent it through my intestines. So, I could only process a small amount of the food I had eaten at a time while the excess sat at the very top of my stomach waiting to migrate downward into the digestive cycle. But in the meantime, I was doubled over in discomfort. And worse, I was at serious risk of vomiting. The problem with vomiting is that once it started, the chain reaction would not stop until my stomach completely purged itself. Then I would have to wait for the strain to subside and, with an empty stomach again, go back through my re-nourishing process all over again. I had been through this before and it could take up to 24 hours to feel right if the vomiting happened.

I berated myself for coming so far just to ruin all my progress over a single plate of Shepherd's pie. I had 14 hours before the wrestling would start.

So, I took a long walk. I didn't want to run on the treadmill. But the walk accelerated my metabolism just enough for me to go to the bathroom. This cleared the jam and enabled more of the food from the top of my stomach to descend into the pit of my stomach and the discomfort started to wane.

By the time I shut off the light and hit the pillow, I felt halfway recovered from my fatal mistake. It still hurt to lay on my stomach in a certain position. But I could feel the digestion kick in and by the morning, I felt much better.

My stomach righted itself. My muscles had absorbed a good amount of the water I drank. My face filled out. And best of all, I was hungry for breakfast. I took a much more restrained approach to eating breakfast and made my way to the arena feeling more well-fed, better nourished, super hydrated and energetic than I had in several months.

I had dotted the "i" and crossed the "t" of my Headlock journey and had no other objective left than to go out to the mat and compete to the best of my ability.

17

I had one guy to beat. The weight class consisted of me and one other competitor. He hailed from Minnesota and had placed fourth in the much bigger Freestyle National Championship tournament the previous year.

I watched him warm up and he didn't look any better than me. I tuned him out and focused on preparing myself mentally and physically. I ran around the stadium. I dropped for 20 push-ups. I bounced up and down. I stretched my legs, groin, arms and neck. I worked a sweat and felt my blood flow. I recalled my wrestling career and replayed the highlights in my head. I reminded myself of all my best moves and visualized them as I jogged in place.

There were 12 bouts scheduled ahead of mine and I stood by the side of the mat watching these former Division I standouts battle each other. Some of the wrestlers impressed me. Some blew me away. Some looked beatable. I couldn't wait to hit the mat.

I looked at my dad in the expansive bleachers along the 10-yard line of the football field with his iPad ready to record my match. I thought fondly of his unwavering devotion throughout high school and college where he faithfully videotaped all my matches. Here we were, 25 or 30 years later, 1,500 miles away from home and still at it.

The past 16 months, the 650 miles I ran, the sweets I sacrificed, the 10,000 push-ups and sit-ups, all converged to contribute to the singular moment when I stepped onto the mat in my plain black singlet and shiny new headgear.

We shook hands. The ref blew the whistle. The part of the story that I thought would fall into place did not go as planned. We tied up. His arms gripped mine like iron vices. Again, I faced another opponent who dwarfed my strength. I had quickness and better mat sense. But I struggled to escape from his grip when he clamped my arms.

I made a mistake. I tried too hard to extricate myself from his grip and loosen enough space to try and score on him. I had an overhook with my right arm and just needed to free my underhook arm to attempt my headlock on him. With 10 or 12 seconds to go in the period, if I threw it and missed, I could scramble to avoid giving up the takedown, maybe roll out of bounds and keep the score level at 0-0.

Instead, I struggled enough to tip myself slightly off balance and raise my head a hair too high.

With eight seconds left in the period, he hit me with a headlock of his own. His technique was not nearly as fluid or graceful as mine, but what he lacked in mechanics, he more than made up in brute force. I thought for a moment, as I felt my body twist and descend to the mat, that I could stop it. However, he pulled it off and made the move work. With the headlock, he scored a two-point takedown and three additional points for exposing a portion of my back to the mat for greater than five seconds.

I never expected to yield the headlock. It's my move - damnit. I almost never give it up to an opponent. But then again, I had wrestled only six matches in the past 20 years. So, anticipating my own patterns, tendencies, limits and abilities had only sparing accuracy and predictability.

Apparently because of our advanced age, the periods in the Veterans Division were shorter than in typical wrestling matches. I saw this as a disadvantage since I had worked myself into such impeccable shape and would be able to outlast opponents who might be more likely to tire as the match progressed into the late end of the third period. I had beaten so many opponents in the third period throughout my wrestling career, specifically due to my usually high endurance and fitness and often with a last second "Hail Mary" headlock.

However, losing by the score of 5-0 with an abbreviated amount of time to bridge the gap against an accomplished and exceptionally strong wrestler such as my opponent proved too much of a disadvantage to overcome. We wrestled evenly throughout the second and third periods and I lost 6-1. The five-point move exposing my back during the first period created the rift between my one point and his six.

The shorter periods placed a higher premium on each point, especially against such a slow, methodical plodder as this opponent.

I didn't feel tired after the match, but my arms throbbed from straining to overcome his grip. I needed to think through what went wrong and how to beat him in the second match. Down 1-0 in a best of three wrestle-off, I couldn't lose another match, or the tournament would end for me.

The returning National Champion in the 138-pound weight class tapped me on the shoulder and congratulated me on a well-fought match. He told me he thought I could win, but that I couldn't look for a throw. I would have to shoot for his legs and stay out of his upper body tie-up. He was just too strong and could muscle me to the mat at my slightest misstep.

"Just don't give up the big move and you're right there against him," he said.

It felt great to have a returning national champion watch me wrestle, provide some analysis and advice and then encourage me in my next match. I took his words to heart. As much as I had pictured myself throwing glorious headlocks and pinning opponents in crushing high octane moves, the loss reminded me that this was the National Championship and not a Division III dual meet against Bridgewater State or the local Connecticut State Nutmeg Games.

I hadn't just set a goal to compete. I reached for the absolute highest rung of the ladder that I could. And along the way, I reached every goal I sought. I lost the weight. I trained myself to run 10-13 miles at a time. I increased my meager strength to the best of my ability and I wrestled in a variety of challenging situations. I beat a 20-year-old wrestler to place third in Connecticut and I scored on several of the guys from my college when I worked out with them.

All my objectives had fallen into place for me. And, while I had to work hard to accomplish what I did, I experienced success at every turn. I dropped from 201 to 167. Then I reset my goal to 152 and 138, eventually getting all the way down to a ridiculously low 125.4.

In the second match, he took me down to take a 2-0 lead, but I felt more confident than I had in the previous match. I managed to reverse control and take the top position from him. I wrestled a smart match and equaled him move for move. I entered the second period with a 4-2 advantage. But he managed to smack me with another five-point move, exposing my back to the mat and retaking the lead, 7-4. I'd love to say I made another mistake. But to his credit, my opponent showed great technique and used his overpowering strength to make it work. I had to fight for an entire minute - a virtual eternity in wrestling time - to avoid allowing him to pin both of my shoulders to the mat for the win.

I had a productive third period, completely dominating him from the top position. I worked a power half nelson with double grapevines, which consists of my legs wrapped around his with my hips trapping his flush to the mat. With his lower body immobilized, I cranked his head sideways, rotating his upper body toward his back and scored two points to up the score to 7-6, one point away from tying the match.

After earning my points, I worked the same move a second time. I pressured his lower body. I punished his head and torqued his neck. His shoulders rotated as they had previously. He let out a gruesome moan and exhaled. I applied all the strength I could. He groaned again. His back edged toward the mat in increments of tiny nudges at a time. I could hear his coach calling out the seconds left in the third and final period.

"20 seconds," he called out. "Ten seconds... Five seconds..."

I needed to move him one more inch, maybe another 5-degree angle to earn two additional points and take an 8-7 lead. He bent, but didn't break. The time ran out. I lost 7-6. My dream to win the national championship would have to wait.

18

Did your parents ever tell you that you could "be whatever you wanted to be"? Or that you could accomplish "anything that you set your mind to accomplishing"? Did you believe them?

You should.

I spent 16 months preparing myself and training for an accomplishment that I had dreamed about since I was 17-years-old. My ultimate objective was to become a NATIONAL CHAMPION at the USA Wrestling Master Nationals.

I competed to the absolute best of my ability. I didn't win the National Championship. I lost in the finals by the score of 7-6. Down 7-4 with a minute left, I scored two points to get within one. With ten seconds left, I came within an inch of scoring two more points. Had I had five or 10 more seconds, I'm convinced I would have turned him to his back to earn the winning points. But he successfully held me off and preserved the victory and I settled for second place.

I had set a plan in January, 2016 to eat healthier, whip myself into shape, build my strength and start working out on the wrestling mat again. In the 1980's and 90's, I had wrestled in High School and College and for several years after college in regional and national level tournaments. But, as a 48-year-old pudgy dad, it had been nearly 20 years since I had competed at that level in the sport that I loved.

I weighed 201 pounds and could barely run a mile.

So, as motivation to improve myself, I set a vision and a goal to compete in the tournament. I had hoped to lose 25 pounds to 167 and my only objective was to compete effectively.

But during the year, by setting daily objectives and simultaneously staying focused on my big expectations, I achieved my initial benchmark much sooner than expected. As I progressed, I continuously reset my expectations higher. I decided to drop to the 152-pound class and then all the way to 138. By the time I arrived in Iowa, my ambition landed far above what I originally thought possible. Eventually, I developed a Big Vision, a Bold Strategy and a Brave Approach to lose 75 pounds down to the 127-pound class and not just to compete admirably, but to win.

I created six distinct plans and dedicated myself to each one:

1. **The Food Plan**: Eating healthy, nutritious food every day & eliminating needless calories.
2. **The Exercise Plan**: Running 60 miles a month and working out to raise my overall fitness.
3. **The Strength Plan**: Building the muscle to compete including 10,000 push-ups in one year.
4. **The Measurement Plan**: Reviewing weight, mileage and strength milestones every day.
5. **The Disclosure Plan**: Sharing goals with my network to create pressure & drive motivation.
6. **The Workout Plan**: Practicing skills and building toughness in live wrestling environments.

I awoke every morning thinking about the steps I needed to take that day to move forward toward my objective. And I went to bed each night reflecting on how well I accomplished what I needed to do as well as where I needed to place my efforts the next day. This level of intense, constant focus on daily objectives enabled these plans to succeed.

As a result, I lost 75 pounds from 201 to 125. I dropped from a 36-inch waist to a 28-inch. I ran 650 miles and completed more than 10,000 push-ups and sit-ups in just over one year. I trained with my old high school and college teams. And I competed in local tournaments against 20-year-old college wrestlers, placing third in the Connecticut Nutmeg State Games at 145-pounds. The efforts paid off and I accomplished my original objective to compete in the National Championship.

In fact, I exceeded my objective by wrestling so well and by coming within one or two points of winning the National Championship.

So, yes, when your parents tell you that you can "be whatever you want to be"? Or that you can accomplish "anything that you set your mind to accomplishing"? Believe them. I became a better person for the journey I took. And whether I scored six points to lose by one or eight points to win by one hardly seems like the point of the story any more. The bigger picture is the health, fitness and self-satisfaction achieved along the way as well as the esteem from my peers, the respect from my family and my own sense of tranquility that I pushed the boundaries of my own human capacity and capabilities so far that I even surprised myself.

Plus, they hold the National Championship tournament every year. So, as my parents have said, I still can be what I ultimately want to be; a NATIONAL CHAMPION. It just might take a new Headlock pact with myself, another 12 months and maybe 1,000 miles or 20,000 more push-ups to get there.

Made in the USA
Coppell, TX
13 January 2021